The World of
Donald McGill

*On the whole, human beings
want to be good, but not too good,
and not quite all the time.*
GEORGE ORWELL

*I am quite sure that a hundred years
from now the cards of Donald McGill will
be treasured by collectors and laughed at by that
far more generous race of non-collectors — because
they are often funny, sometimes witty, and
ever so seldom perceptively wise.*
A. CALDER-MARSHALL

The World of Donald McGill

Elfreda Buckland

Javelin Books

POOLE · DORSET

First published in the UK 1984 by Blandford Press,
Link House, West Street, Poole, Dorset BH15 1LL

Reprinted 1985 by Javelin Books

Distributed in the United States by
Sterling Publishing Co., Inc.,
2 Park Avenue, New York, N.Y. 10016.

British Library Cataloguing in Publication Data

Buckland, Elfreda
  The world of Donald McGill.
  1. McGill, Donald
  I. Title
  769.92'4   NC1879.M3/

ISBN 0 7137 1400 X Hardback
ISBN 0 7137 1731 9 Paperback

Typeset by Megaron Typesetting
Colour origination by Apperley Graphics
Reproduced, printed and bound in Great Britain by
Hazell Watson & Viney Limited,
Member of the BPCC Group,
Aylesbury, Bucks

Contents

Acknowledgements

My husband, Basil N. Buckland, has fired me with his long-standing interest in McGill and his co-operation has been an essential ingredient.

I would like to thank all who have given me help in the preparation of this book, particularly Donald McGill's daughters, Mrs. M. R. Tumber, and Mrs. M. E. S. Procter; Michael Tickner, FRSA, FRPS, who helped to start it all; Les Coleman, Robert Scott, Ray Collier and numerous other collectors and postcard dealers.

I would also like to thank Danielle and Stewart Borrett, Anthony Byatt, Neil Rhind, Roger Page-Symonds, May Hunter, Bernie Cornish and Roy Wilson, Miss M. F. Jupe of Swanage, Christine Bayliss; librarians and archivists countrywide; the Isle of Man Censoring Committee; John Henty and John Hayward of Brighton; Ann Atkin of the Gnome Reserve, Doink; the Director and staff of the London Postal Museum; Town Hall staffs; the Swanage Postmaster; Phillips, Sothebys, Stanley Gibbons, Sanders of Oxford, and the directors and staff of Garnet Langton; D. Constance Ltd, Arthur Dixon Ltd and other postcard publishers and retailers; and my two editors, Roy Gasson and Felicity Carter.

Introduction

Donald Fraser Gould McGill – born 1875 – became a legend in his own lifetime. When he died in 1962 his name and familiar signature were already synonymous with the comic postcard. His was the popular art form known to millions of ordinary people. At one and the same time he was a courteous Victorian gentleman of impeccable background and acknowledged 'King of the Saucy Postcards' – 'The Ace of Cards'.

There have been other artists producing comic drawings – Tom Browne, Phil May, Douglas Tempest, Arnold Taylor and Lawson Wood, for instance, but Donald McGill is the rare artist whose name became a trademark and whose works received an accolade from George Orwell in 1941, as examples of 'genuine folk art'. Arthur Calder-Marshall made a serious study of McGill's comic cards in *Wish You Were Here* published in 1966. McGill's work featured in the Brighton Festival of 1967, and with the centenary of his birth in 1975 there was a flurry of renewed interest in him by the media. The occasional Sotheby's sale of any of McGill's original paintings usually results in a further re-examination of his work. It also reveals the enthusiasm of serious postcard collectors, and the interest of artists and social historians in the work, as well as the strength of nostalgia in an electronic age.

Donald McGill, an extraordinary combination of serious student and renowned humorist, would have appreciated a final ironic joke. In 1977 his place amongst 'The Great and the Good' was recognised by no less a respectable organisation than the Greater London Council. One of their coveted blue plaques now marks the large Victorian house at 5 Bennett Park, Blackheath where he lived from 1931-39. Donald McGill spent the greater part of his life in the Greenwich/Blackheath area; he was an outwardly conventional family man. One can see from the photograph that Bennett Park was built for solid middle-class families. The road is wide and tree-lined. It is flanked by substantial four-storeyed houses. Number 5 has the typical 1870's Victorian servants' basement. McGill's neighbours knew little of his daily work but this area undoubtedly had its share of people related to his stock characters. These were houses with parlourmaids, nannies and charladies. Inquisitive tradesmen called, no doubt when the master was out and, or course, it had its share of city gents, policemen, curious postmen and innocent clergy.

The blue plaque ceremony was somewhat unusual. Young men in striped blazers and straw boaters paraded outside McGill's old home, together with scantily-clad bathing belles, saucy maids, crestfallen curates and the sort of red-nosed characters which McGill had made his own. When the great moment for the unveiling arrived the usual blue velvet curtains had been replaced by a pair of frilly Edwardian bloomers! The *Evening News* reported it as 'London's frilly tribute to a cheeky artist'. The *Daily Express* called it, 'A salute in falling bloomers for the sauciest artist of all'. *The Times* thought the blue plaque was 'just the right gesture'. McGill's two daughters disapproved of the bloomers but admitted that their father would have been amused. Television and radio accounts of the ceremony on the 20 September 1977, were either cut or shortened so that the waiting world could receive news of Victor, the mating giraffe, who died at Marwell Zoo on that day. Whilst McGill, with his interest in biology, would no doubt have mourned Victor's death, McGill, the humorist would have joked about the fact that his delayed centenary celebration was ousted from the national news by a splay-legged giraffe!

1
Donald McGill -His Own World

Almost every journalist's column on McGill starts from George Orwell's well-known essay written for the magazine *Horizon* in 1941, 'The Art of Donald McGill'. Apart from any other value which can be attributed to his words, Orwell admits that he doesn't know exactly who McGill is: 'He is apparently a trade name, for at least one series of postcards is issued simply as the Donald McGill Comics, but he is unquestionably a real person, with a style of drawing recognisable at a glance.' Orwell was profoundly right in one sense and deeply wrong in another. It is true that the work of Donald McGill is instantly recognisable and quite distinct from his later and cruder imitators. To suggest that he was a brand name or a team, as writers were in the named columns of the national press with which Orwell was familiar, was far off the mark. Donald McGill was one man, a very special man, and this book attempts to put his life's work in context.

The Victorian Gentleman

Donald Fraser Gould McGill certainly was a real person. He was born on 25 January 1875 at Regent's Park — he often joked about the fact that his birthplace was near the monkey cage in Regent's Park Zoo and said '— it was pure luck I was outside the cage'. He lived to become the doyen of the comic postcard industry and was still producing designs for cards well into his eighties. He died in 1962 at the age of 87 — with the designs for 1963 already prepared!

He was justly proud of his ancestry which reflected respectability rather than the ribaldry that is associated with him. After the death of his wife in 1952 he made a long-promised visit to Scotland, the McGill homeland. He allocated time to checking and completing the family tree which had been prepared by his youngest brother Herbert. His ancestors were originally yeoman farmers and he traced a McGill back to 1660. In his will he specifically mentions his family papers, documents, portraits and letters, and earnestly hoped that they would be preserved.

Arthur Calder-Marshall in *Wish You Were Here* points out that one of the clan, Dr William McGill, D.D. (1732-1807) of Carsenestock, wrote an essay which created sufficient stir for Robert Burns to feature him as the Doctor Mac in a satirical ballad called 'The Kirk's Alarm'.

Donald McGill stayed at Newton Stewart and discovered that his great-great-grandfather, William McGill (1720-1802), of nearby Auchland, Wigtown, was a pillar of the Church of Scotland. His son the Hon. John McGill (1752-1834) left Auchland for Virginia in 1773. He served first in the Loyal Virginians and subsequently as a Captain in the Queen's Rangers. Donald McGill carefully preserved the claymore which John McGill, his great-great-uncle, carried during the American War of Independence and bequeathed it to his grandson. He saw himself as part of a lineage which was not afraid to rebel or take a minority view. For instance, he was a considered atheist when this was not a popular stance; he supported the suffragettes and embraced Liberal politics.

John McGill finally settled in Toronto, Canada where he obtained high office. The founding of the new province of Upper Canada gave him the opportunity to exert his considerable administrative skills. He became a member of the Executive Council in 1796 and later, in 1813, Receiver General. Having no heirs he persuaded his nephew Peter McCutcheon, whose branch of the family had originally come from Newton Stewart, and who was Donald McGill's grandfather, to take the name of Peter McGill in 1821.

The McGill's were prominent in Canadian society. Another clansman, the Hon. James McGill (1744-1813), had founded McGill College. It was modelled on non-sectarian, liberal principles and by its charter of 31 March 1821 it attained recognised University status. Inaugurated in 1829, Peter McGill, formerly Peter McCutcheon, was an active Life Governor and trustee from 1832. Following his uncle's example he also distinguished himself in public office, becoming Mayor of Montreal in 1840-42 and President of the Montreal Bank for 26 years from 1834-60. He was a member, (1832-60), and Speaker in 1847 of the Legislative Council of Canada and, in addition, became President of the Board of Trade in 1848.

Captain John Shuter Davenport McGill, James McGill's son and Donald's father, was born in Montreal in 1834. He served as a Lieutenant in the 60th Royal Rifles – the K.R.R.C. during the Indian Mutiny. The pencil sketch of him was made at Delhi Palace in 1857. He was one of the officers who mounted guard over the ex-king of Delhi and his family. He was only 23 when this drawing was made; the beard makes him look older. Perhaps he has a certain aristocratic look. The pipe and the book give him a relaxed air in spite of the military decorations. Notwithstanding the victory at Delhi the army held no permanent attraction for him and two years after this sketch was made, when he was only 25, he relinquished his commission. He had inherited enough money from investments and property, and from the McGill fur-trading activities in Canada, to settle in this country and live in some style at Pilgrims Hall, Brentwood, Essex.

Unfortunately, John McGill's financial judgement did not match that of his father and his great-uncle. He made a series of disastrous investments and by 1883 was forced to find some way of restoring the family fortunes. Shortly after successfully applying to become secretary of Poplar Hospital, he caught a chill and died of pleurisy when he was only 49. He left his widow with seven children and an income steadily reducing in value. It was sufficient however to enable her to move into a new house in St John's Park, Blackheath, Kent in 1886.

Donald McGill's mother was a Miss Rosina Bisgood, born in 1840. She was the youngest of the eight children of Thomas Bisgood a solicitor of Ampthill Square in north-west London. He practised on his own account at 36 Carey Street, London WC, until he was joined by his son in 1857. Just how Rosina Bisgood met John Shuter Davenport McGill is lost in the mists of time. Like many Victorian contemporaries Rosina married early when she was only 18, in 1859. Between 1860 and 1881 she produced a large family of nine children – five boys and four girls, of whom seven survived. Her grand-daughter remembers that she was very sweet and very smart. From the time her husband died she wore black, the traditional Victorian widow's weeds, and a little white lace cap on her head. In keeping with the times she spoiled her four sons and expected her three daughters to wait on them. She kept a maid and her grand-daughters loved to stay with her; one of the attractions was that they were served tea and biscuits in bed in the morning.

Mrs McGill had very definite views; her grand-daughters remember taking a long detour rather than risk being seen by granny on their way to the tennis courts on a Sunday morning. There was nothing of the fragile Victorian lady about Rosina. Despite being widowed for 52 years and mothering her large family, she lived to be 95.

Donald grew up with his three surviving brothers and three unmarried sisters. It is interesting to note that the whole family could draw. In fact, in Donald McGill's opinion, the work of one of his sisters was very good indeed. His spinster sisters protected and cared for his mother. Undoubtedly they gave him some insight into the spinster's plight and this was later to become one of his popular themes. These may seem cruel jokes, and no doubt McGill's cards which fall into this category would be labelled sexist by today's feminists, but they reflected the reality of their time. For many hundreds of women 'making a match' was their only hope of respect and financial security. The quest for a suitable husband loomed large. The war, the preponderance of surviving female children and the demands of an expanded Empire resulted by 1921 in a 'surplus' of 1¾ million women.

Despite the size of the family, his brother Duncan was sent to the Merchant Taylors' School and Donald first attended Stratheden House and later, in 1890, Blackheath Proprietary School. The latter took boys from the age of eight and had an excellent reputation. It had stood on the corner of what was Lee Lane (now Lee Terrace) and Blackheath Village since October 1831.

Neil Rhind in his study of *Blackheath Village and Environs 1790-1970* quotes *The Standard* of 1869 which describes the village as 'not exactly of the rustic order . . . we doubt whether a thatched roof, a hayrick or a pigsty could be found in all the place. The windows of the houses, we dare not call them cottages, are festooned with muslin and shaded by venetians. The gardens have the choicest of flowers and in the highways are the most elegant of shops – of the villagers it may be said that they walk in silk attire . . . and not infrequently vary their outdoor enjoyments by riding instead of walking. Blackheath is a village of the upper middle-class', and it continued so to be.

The Blackheath Proprietary School was founded to cater for the sons of this same class. It was in a rapidly growing, desirable area − near enough to London to enable papa to reach the centres of commerce and industry, the stock exchange, the law courts and Parliament − but rural enough, with its heath and open spaces, to provide a healthy atmosphere for the growing family. The name Blackheath Proprietary School, often confused with 'preparatory' and 'propriety', was taken because the school was owned by share-holding proprietors who contributed one hundred £20 shares to the initial capital. The idea proved to be so successful it was copied by Cheltenham College in 1841. No proprietor was to have more than three £20 shares and could nominate one scholar for each share. The fact that Donald was nominated as a scholar by an East Indian merchant, Henry Tolputt, explains why he did not join his elder brother Duncan at the Merchant Taylors' School.

The objects of the 'Prop', as it became known, were to provide an education, described in J. W. Kirby's history of the school, as one which would include 'Classical Learning, the Modern Languages, Maths, Reading, Writing, History, Geography and such other branches of modern Science and General Literature as may be conveniently introduced − together with religious and moral instruction in conformity with the doctrines and disciplines of the

Church of England'. Donald McGill came under the influence of one of its great teachers F. Osiander, a native of Wurtemberg. The calibre of such staff and the breadth of the curriculum helped to establish McGill's lifelong academic interests.

The 'Prop' closed in December 1907 but the Old Boys' connection lived on, reduced in the end to a small group, still in touch in the early 1970s.

Kirby, quoting from the Blackheath Local Guide on the club's bi-annual dinner in 1939 reports, 'In the history of public schools it must be unique for an old boys' club to be flourishing with four hundred members after the school had been closed down for over 30 years.' Donald McGill supported the old Blackheathans' Club. After the Second World War he attended every annual dinner until his death in 1962, bound by what *The Times* called 'a most prehensile old school tie'. Nevertheless, he could still make jokes about the latter, (*See plate 1*). Ironically, the demolition of the old school and the building on the site of a block of flats, Selwyn Court, was one of the factors which led to the founding of the Blackheath Society and the Preservation Trust Ltd, the aims of which struck a sympathetic chord in McGill.

Donald enjoyed his schooldays and did not find the work difficult. His younger daughter thinks he 'should have become a teacher because he always explained things so well – but he was mad about

18

sport.' I note from school records that hockey was offered to boys whose parents thought rugby football was 'too dangerous'. Obviously, Rosina McGill did not anticipate just how dangerous the game of rugby would turn out to be for her son. His eagerness to play was to have unexpected and serious consequences. When he was only sixteen he sustained an injury to his left ankle during a rugby match. With a stoicism that was typical, and which was a quality which remained with him throughout his life, he finished the match and subsequently made little of the incident. He suffered considerable pain in the months which followed and by the time he was prevailed upon to see a doctor the damaged bone in his foot was so diseased that he finally had to have his foot amputated. For weeks he had to be pushed about in a wheelchair before he was eventually fitted with an artificial limb. This he coped with so well that many did not detect his disability. His housekeeper in later life, Mrs Margaret Gordon coming upon him unexpectedly, witnessed him fitting on his artificial foot and was taken completely by surprise. It is almost worthy of a McGill-type joke for he subsequently left her most of his household effects. One can imagine the caption – 'Man with wooden leg gives all to astonished housekeeper.' Not that anyone would have thought of Donald Fraser Gould McGill behaving at any time other than with total propriety. He confessed to feeling 'somewhat embarrassed' at his housekeeper's inadvertent intrusion.

He generally made no issue of his loss and walked without a limp, even though as he grew older he suffered severe pain in his left leg. Nevertheless, in an interview with Eric Smithfield for *John Bull* in August 1949, when he was 74, he maintained that the replacement for his foot 'was so good I was able to play three seasons as scrum-half with the old Victoria Club at Blackheath'. Was Smithfield having his leg pulled?

He left Blackheath 'Prop' in 1891 and since he had a 'flair for artistic work' he attended the Art School founded in Bennett Park, Blackheath in 1881. This was an independent school recognised by the Government schools in South Kensington. His mother hoped that he would eventually gain an Arts and Crafts Teacher's certificate but he left after a year because, according to his elder daughter, he did not like the syllabus. 'He wanted to do caricatures and there was too much painting of flowers.' In his spare time he drew for the newsletters of the local sports clubs.

He started his career by joining a firm of naval architects, Maudsleys, in London, where he stayed for three years from 1893-1896. He then became articled as an engineering draughtsman to the reconstructed Thames Ironworks, Shipbuilding and Engineering Company. He finished his apprenticeship with the firm and stayed until 1907.

Enthusiasts and critics often refer to the workmanlike draughtsmanship of McGill's drawings (*see plates 2, 3 and 4*). The discipline of his early training remained with him throughout his life. Reginald Pound, former editor of *Strand Magazine*, discussed McGill and his comic cards in a book *Maypole in the Strand*, published in 1948. He felt that McGill had the air of a retired naval commander and relished the fact that at his Old Boys' Dinners he liked to sit next to the Bishop of Wakefield, his old school chum. Some may think this an unlikely liaison but it was genuine. McGill has been variously described as looking like a solicitor, judge or church warden.

Even in the court cells at Lincoln awaiting an obscenity charge related to his postcard designs, his solicitor described him as 'serene'. In July 1954, in an interview with Robert Jackson for the magazine *Illustrated* he described himself as being '. . . rather Victorian in outlook'. He certainly dressed impeccably, even at the drawing board. Words like 'spry' and 'dapper' were being applied to him when he was in his 80's and still working.

Donald McGill's life seems full of contradictions. The area of Greenwich and Blackheath where he lived was culturally rich. According to Neil Rhind there were soirées, musical evenings, art exhibitions of high standard, charity concerts, bazaars and dancing classes in the area, but it was from the former old Crowder's Music Hall, in what was then Stockwell Street, Greenwich that McGill plucked his bride.

Florence Isabel Hurley was one of three daughters of Alfred Ambrose Hurley, the proprietor and manager of the music hall and the adjoining public house, the Rose and Crown, from 1878 until 1900, the year his daughter was married. It was rumoured that he started his working life in the Bank of England. Be that as it may, he was a man of some vision. He renamed the music hall of Charles Spencer Crowder 'The Royal Borough Theatre of Varieties'. His predecessor had tried to give the old music hall a veneer of respectability by offering an entertainment 'of high moral character' to the inmates of the Greenwich workhouse. His offer was politely declined by the Board of Guardians but subsequently Alfred Ambrose Hurley advertised, 'Three hours and a half refined and rational entertainment without vulgarity'. A footnote points out that the hall was open on Sunday evenings for 'Professional Re-union and Social Conversazione'. In fact it became famous for its Sunday evening performances by seamen ashore from the ships moored at Greenwich. A lively music hall programme was also maintained with singers, dancers, acrobats, jugglers, comics, clog dancers, and an annual pantomine.

Florence's father had a great influence on the development of the Greenwich Music Hall. The population of Greenwich was increasing and in an attempt to lure in the better educated the name of the music hall was changed in the 1880's to the more refined 'Parthenon Theatre of Varieties'. There was competition from neighbouring music halls but Donald's father-in-law not only rebuilt the Rose and Crown in 1895 but, in 1898, he gave the music hall a splendid new façade which lasted until 1960. The name was changed once more to 'The Hippodrome'. The lively Greenwich Theatre has occupied the site since 1970.

Florence Isabel lived above the Rose and Crown. She was well acquainted with the bustle, the life, the stars and the acts which pulled in the crowds. One wonders what McGill's mother, 60 years old when Donald married, thought of the liaison between her son, with his aristocratic and military background and the daughter of Alfred Ambrose Hurley. Of course, Alfred Hurley was a man of some distinction in Greenwich. He rode around the district in a pony and trap, wore a bowler and a buttonhole and was always referred to, in the traditional music hall term, as the 'Guv'nor'. Nevertheless it is unlikely that he moved in the same social circle as the McGills. No doubt some eyebrows were raised. One can imagine the effect on McGill's three spinster sisters.

Both McGill's daughters remember their mother with great affection. 'She was good-tempered, a really lovely person who never said an unkind word.' She had a flair for fashion and was a liberating influence on the family. 'She worked hard and always told us to make the most of ourselves.' She was 'very respectable and never went out without gloves and a hat.' Respectability was much prized in late-Victorian times. It is the most over-worked word in the situations vacant columns of the *Kentish Mercury* published soon after the McGills married: 'Wanted, respectable young person for the general work of the house', 'Wanted, respectable girl as general', 'Wanted, a respectable young man as carman.' The advertisers had to prove their respectability also: 'Wanted by respectable person – a cook.'

Florence Isabel Hurley had to cope with these prim, Victorian pressures. It was fortunate that McGill loved the music hall. That was where his romance blossomed. It was the music hall which was the background to Florence's life until she married. It provides the most obvious connection between McGill's art and his life. He loved the bawdy, rumbustious humour and this was reflected in his cards. When one looks at his gallery of fat ladies, amiable drunks, weedy husbands, aggressive ma's-in-law, naive parsons, canny Scots and his risqué *double entendre* one might be forgiven for imagining that he must have been some sort of ebullient 'Cheeky Chappie', like Max Miller. The facts belie the illusion. Robert Jackson writing for *Illustrated* in 1954 called him, 'a precise and elegant artist'. Up to his death at 87, he was described as modest and courteous with a soft, cultured voice. The author has evidence from his staff' and the company solicitor that he was 'a perfect gentleman'. Anyone reading his letters becomes aware of his elegant hand and his innate courtesy even under quite stressful conditions, when the business with which he had been associated for virtually the whole of his life was patently failing.

Apart from a brief period which he spent as a temporary clerk with the Ministry of Labour at Guildford during the Second World War, he derived the whole of his income between 1908-1962 from designing postcards.

Fatherhood he took seriously. The elder daughter, born in May 1901, was named after her redoubtable grandmother, Mary Rosina. The younger daughter was born in November 1904. To her name, Margaret Elizabeth, was added one of her grandfather's names, Shuter. McGill saw to it that his two daughters were educated, and supported them when they expressed a wish to acquire secretarial qualifications. They both married well, the elder one to Lt. Col. C. Tumber,

OBE – a lecturer in Military Science at an army school – and the younger one to a highly qualified engineer, Robert Procter. The Procter family emigrated to South Africa for 17 years after the Second World War and McGill's two grandsons were educated at Michaelhouse, South Africa's exclusive public school. The older boy inherited his grandfather's artistic ability – though he does not exploit it. He has passed it on to his young daughter. It is heartening to think that something of Donald McGill's unique talent, survives. Having visited both of McGill's daughters I found them looking surprisingly bright and young for their age. Mrs Tumber assured me that their youthful good looks and humour were a McGill characteristic. She was still driving at 82 and said with a laugh, 'The McGills have always had all their buttons.' No doubt of this.

McGill confessed in July 1957 on a TV programme 'This Week' that his saucy postcards were best sellers in the trade – 'vulgar sometimes, but just a bit of fun.'

Nevertheless he was mindful of his married daughters' sensibilities. They 'ran like stags whenever they passed a comic postcard shop,' he said. Although by then quite famous – considered a worthy propagator of the broad, earthy English humour found in Chaucer, Shakespeare, Hogarth and Dickens – he sometimes kept his occupation, 'a bit dark,' to protect them.

Donald McGill's intellectual capacity can be gauged by the range of his interests. These included medicine, biology, astrology, anthropology and cricket. Whilst spending his working days designing thousands of comic cards, his leisure time was spent in his library studying his favourite subject – anthropology. He maintained that this area of study, 'Gives you a sense of perspective'. Already well known by 1949, his natural modesty nevertheless revealed itself in an interview with Eric Smithfield for the magazine *John Bull*. 'Anthropology,' he said, 'makes you realise you're no more than a blade of grass.'

Towards the end of his life he admitted somewhat regretfully in a television interview, 'I'm not proud of myself, I always wanted to do something better. I'm really a serious minded man underneath – I would have liked to have done sporting caricatures like Tom Webster or even oil paintings, if I'd had my way.'

How did this modest, courtly Victorian gentleman enter the blatantly vulgar, some would say, 'bizarre' world of comic cards?

2
First Steps as a Postcard Artist

On Donald McGill's birth certificate his father's profession is given as 'stationer' and one might assume from this that it was through the good offices of his father that McGill became associated with the postcard industry. This was not the case since Donald was only eight years old when his father died. His introduction to the postcard world came later when he was nearly 30. He must have had some misgivings about leaving the safe well-ordered life of an engineering draughtsman to make an inauspicious debut into the postcard world, particularly since he was, by the end of 1904, a family man with two small daughters. One was a baby and the other only three-years-old. Nevertheless, McGill's timing proved to be fortuitous, coinciding as it did with the blossoming postcard industry. 419 million cards had been posted at the turn of the century and by 1914 this figure had grown to 880 million.

McGill's incursion into the postcard world came in 1904 through his brother, who had admired a humorous sketch which Donald had made on the back of a postcard. He had sent it to cheer up his nephew who was in hospital with diptheria. The sentiment expressed was, 'Hope you'll soon be out,' but it was illustrated with a drawing of a man holding a notice which warned 'No Skating', as he tried to struggle from an icy pond. The humour was original and immediate. With his brother's encouragement Donald began to draw cards in his spare time for Max Honnest-Reddlich a newspaper reporter and founder of The Pictorial Postcard Company, of German extraction. His introduction to the postcard world was not as haphazard as one has been led to believe. Anthony Byatt in his book *Picture Postcards and their Publishers* points out that McGill's eldest brother John, and John's wife Grace, had ten shares in the newly formed Pictorial Postcard Company. My own research revealed the fact that Grace McGill's sister married Max Honnest-Reddlich.

The subjects of some of the first cards were a long way from the riotous seaside characters which were to dominate the market by the 1930s. One early series illustrated familiar but rather staid Stock Exchange jargon which was nevertheless admired by the stockbrokers of Blackheath. For instance, 'Sugar Falling – small man squeezed' showed a weedy man being felled to the ground by a box of sugar whilst 'Argentine rails going up' pictures a man attempting to stuff a stick of dynamite beneath a railway line. Drawing on his early sporting experiences, these were followed first by football caricatures and later, in 1906, by a set of six cards on cricket. There were cards with captions in short telegram style with an appropriate drawing, e.g. Bertie sends a telegram to his pet barmaid suggesting the Trocadero for a meeting. Below, the picture shows him calling at the pawnbroker to raise the necessary cash. These jokes may now seem like schoolboy humour but by December 1905 the *Picture Postcard Magazine* spoke prophetically of Donald McGill as a young 'humour-artist' whose designs for comic cards 'will soon become widely popular'. There was a version of 'Please Lord, excuse me a minute while I kick Fido' available in 1906. McGill re-worked it in 1916 and it continued to be a best seller until the 1960s. McGill admitted he did not understand why it proved to be so popular. He called it, 'a little gold mine' and had to re-draw it when the blocks wore out. There were three versions showing a small pig-tailed girl kneeling by her bed saying her prayers whilst a puppy playfully tugs at her nightie, exposing her nether regions. The heavy wooden furniture is typical of its day but the colours of the drapes, the linen, the striped green wallpaper, which Lord Kinross said later became known as 'Eccles Regency', in the earlier versions are softer, without the heavy black outline of later postcards. It is estimated that this card – one of the least saucy ones – sold 1½ million copies by 1949, 2 million by 1957 and 3 million by 1962. There is even an early French version of this card which sold well. The caption reads, 'S'il vous plaît, Seigneur; excusez-moi une minute pendant que je donne ma coup de pied à Médor.' On the back of one produced for Inter Arts in 1917, Tom writes from Blackpool to say, 'The children are having a beano and giving me one too. They are giving the donkeys socks and the ice-cream tub. We have seen the winter gardens and the tower.' This missive really gives something of the flavour of the period.

It took McGill time to develop his own distinctive style with the use of bold, bright, primary colours – particularly red becoming dominant. Those of his cards which used softer colours and more detailed drawing have their own charm, such as 'Follow my leader', one of the only set of six story cards McGill drew, also the pipe dream of the man who 'wants a good girl and wants her bad . . .' and the spooning couple who feel that it's dreadful that this is the last evening they shall have together until tomorrow night. *(Plates 5, 6)*.

In *plates 1 & 3* the draughtsman's hand can be seen. There is a fine balance in the one showing a drunken reveller umbrella in hand, collapsed on his bed; jacket, top hat, one boot, yellow gloves discarded.

The caption reads 'The end of a perfect day' and for the French market 'La fin d'une journée parfaite'. The angle of the umbrella and the fallen chair are neatly counterpointed by the top hat. Another well-balanced design shows a rubicund cigar-smoking gentleman in black waistcoat, red tie, grey pinstripes and spats writing a letter. The caption reads 'Please find enclosed ten pounds – I can't'. The slope of the cracked mirror and the angle of the wall draw the eye to the beer bottle at the ready, on the table. Then one notices the clip of bills on the wall, the peeling plaster and a cobweb with dangling spider. Another well drawn card shows a monocled gent complete with shining top hat, yellow waistcoat and gloves – a 'masher' holding a banana. 'Don't swank about your lunch. It's only a banana and a walk round', says the caption. By cleverly inserting a street post, McGill transfixes the man between that, the vertical of the wall and the angle of his umbrella to give him a nervous guilty look as he rounds the corner and raises his banana.

Although Donald McGill's style changed, his method of working did not. The jokes came first – they were all-important. These he heard in the music hall or the pub, read them in newspapers or heard them in general conversation. In his later years he admitted he sometimes adapted 'cracks' from popular radio programmes. If he was really stuck for an idea

TIMESPAN

The Storehouse of Highland History

HELMSDALE · SUTHERLAND
01431 821 327

6 9 25 45 47 48 (814)

13.36

B+B.

01905 | 6837 47 McCallum

0141 | 884 54 33

Sun / Mon. PM.

"The end of a perfect day." La fin d'une journée parfaite.

THE·ORANGE·PEEL·
·CAKE·WALK·

Has it ever occurred to you ?

Donald McGill

DONT SWANK ABOUT YOUR 'LUNCH'

IT'S ONLY 'A BANANA AND A WALK ROUND'.

Please find enclosed ten pounds—I can't!

I WANT A GOOD GIRL...
AND I WANT HER BAD !

6

"How dreadful it seems darling, that this
is the last evening we shall have together
until tomorrow night!"

5

BIRTHDAY WISHES.

FROM THE TIME THE SUN RISES
TILL AT EVENING IT SETS
MAY YOUR BIRTHDAY BE HAPPY
AND LEAVE NO REGRETS
AND AS I'M AFRAID THERE'S NO
CHANCE OF OUR MEETING
I SEND YOU THIS POSTCARD
TO GIVE YOU MY GREETING.

Donald McGill

8

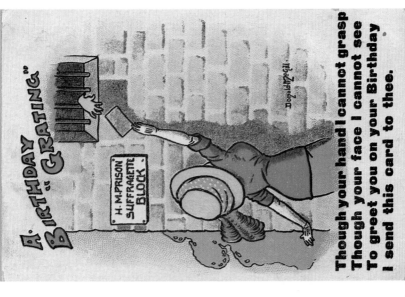

A. BIRTHDAY "GRATING"

H.M.PRISON
SUFFRAGETTE
BLOCK

Donald McGill

Though your hand I cannot grasp
Though your face I cannot see
To greet you on your Birthday
I send this card to thee.

7

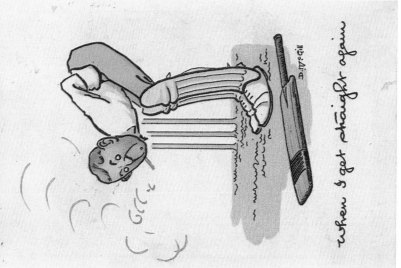

The Woodbury Series. No. 1140.

when I get straight again

D. McGill.

10

D. McGill 1905.

Jnebriated Poet:
..Moons! Moons!! How beautiful is Moons —
all in one radiant an' glorious bunch!!"

9

"Can you give me something to help the Old Ladies' Home?"

"Help 'em home? Why, what have they been up to?"

"I thought I could help you—I saw your predicament."

"Did you? Well, if you were a gentleman you wouldn't mention it."

"Don't mix with those who have too much 'bounce' take it easy!"

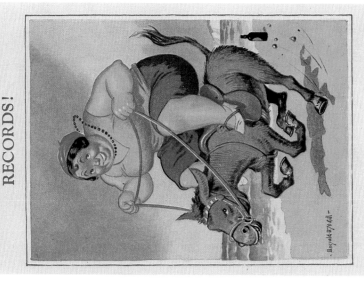

HAVING A WONDERFUL TIME HERE—BEATING ALL RECORDS!

" Please send a woman to share my lot,
No one knows what a lot I've got,
Rich or poor, she'll still be blessed,
Send her along – I'll do the rest ! "

" Please send a man to share my lot,
No one knows what a lot I've got.
Rich or poor he'll still be blessed,
Send him along – I'll do the rest ! "

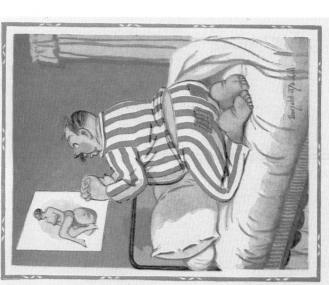

JUST A LINE FROM BLACKPOOL.

19

"So you've been down to Brighton for week, Mr. Topweight.
Got plenty of ozone down there, eh?" "Er — well — you see I had the missis with me!"

20

"There you are! What did I tell you?"

"OH, LORD, IF EVER YOU
WANTS TO SHOW HOW
YOU LOVES LITTLE BOYS
WHAT TRIES HARD TO
BE GOOD — NOW'S
YOUR TIME !!"

Donald McGill.

23

24

THE
SHORTEST
PRAYER
ON RECORD:

—

A MAN,
AMEN!

—

To my Valentine

If I wrote of my love in pages a score
I could only mean one thing —
Just one and no more;
That one little thing takes but one little line
"Say you will be, dear,
my own Valentine!"

Beggols 1741 G.A.

To my Valentine.

If you want a Heart that's warm and true.
A Heart you pick out mine.
It's warmth for you will never cool.
If you'll be my Valentine.

Beggols 1742 G.A.

Dam it, take it if it'll keep you quiet !

I'm looking after my own affairs !

HAVE YOU EVER HEARD
OF THESE THINGS?

IF SO, WHY THE
DONT YOU USE ONE AND
LET ME HEAR FROM YOU!

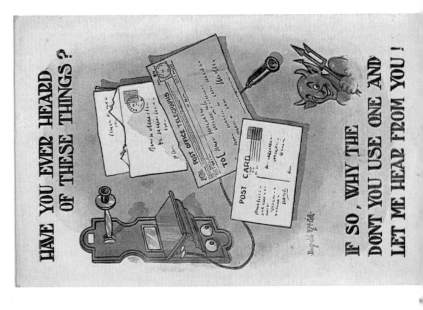

I'M SORRY
I MISSED THE POST!

he would make lists of promising words trying them out for ambiguity, puns and malapropism.

'Did he!' says the nonplussed judge to the smart young girl of 1910. We are left to surmise just what *he* did. The sender of the card seems more certain: 'Do not be late, meet me at the gate, at eight'. 'I am surprised at you — Going on like this,' says Jim to Miss Stewart of Wandsworth. 'A Birthday Grating' shows a card being handed through the prison bars of the suffragette block. Two 1920 charladies chat and one says to the other — 'Yus, the dirty dog ses it was butter but I knoo it was margarine so I popped round to the Town 'all and 'ad it paralyzed by the anarchist'. 'Would you care for a Sonata before dinner?' the musical young lady asks the red nosed Mr Jones. 'Well thank you, I had a couple coming along, but I could do with another small one!' The man rushing forward to pick up the girl who has fallen over a fence says 'I thought I could help you — I saw your predicament.' 'Did you?', she replies, 'Well, if you were a gentleman you wouldn't mention it.' The double entendre moves with the times. Man ogling the beach girl, 'Smart girl too — matriculated when she was 16!' 'Little hussy!' says his wife, 'and doesn't mind owning it either!!'

It was McGill's skill at visually interpreting the joke that was at the heart of his appeal. He would first decide on the caption, then he would draft his original design on pieces of roughly cut board. A line drawing was executed first, then watercolours from an ordinary child's paintbox were used to complete the picture. The artwork was planned to fit within an area which was twice the size of the final postcard. This meant that the proportions and scale of the work took into account the limitations of the size of the finished product. An area 5½in by 3½in (140mm × 89mm) does not provide a broad canvas on which to work. Many of the early postcards were designed by illustrators of magazines like *Punch* and *Vanity Fair*. The more successful of postcards designed for instance by Bert Story, Lance Thackeray, Lawson Wood, John Hassall and Tom Browne took the small size of the card into account. The latter submitted his designs on card which was scaled exactly to the postcard size, so that like McGill's designs, they lost little in reproduction.

Mrs Tumber, McGill's elder daughter, remembers that her father had his 'thinking times' when he was not to be disturbed. He was then working out suitable captions. Apart from these times, he was sometimes lonely working in isolation and the whole family would gather in his room. She remembers reading to him as he painted. His younger daughter remembers that he was what was known then as a 'sport', and was sought out by his nieces and nephews and later by his grandchildren. He had an endearing habit of pulling a face similar to the one he was drawing. He had them all in fits of laughter, played practical jokes and could always make up a ready rhyme to fit any incident or occasion. 'My friends envied my having such a charming Father,' said his elder daughter.

McGill's first efforts sold for six shillings (30p) a time and during the early years he drew about six a week, working as a freelance as well as drawing for the Pictorial Postcard Company. Some of his early cards followed the 'Write-Away' format of Harry Payne which had appeared as early as 1900. An incomplete sentence which the writer could quickly and easily finish was illustrated. One collector has a McGill card postmarked 13 July, 1904 showing a cricketer reaching for a ball, – 'Dear_____ I hope I shall catch you.' A man slipping on a piece of orange peel at the height of the cake-walk craze says 'Has it ever occurred to you . . . ?' There was a sporting series – one shows a cricketer without the benefit of the modern box, doubled up in pain. 'When I get straight again,' says the message, and the sender has added a fag and some smoke. Later, there were numerous versions of 'Just a line . . .'. The line was made up of fatties, beer bottles, large families, fish or animals. Another series used teddy bears which included a suffragette reference with 'Christabear' holding a banner demanding the vote. The inebriate surfaced as early as 1905 – as a poet. 'Moons!

Moons! how beautiful is Moons – all in one radiant an' glorious bunch!!' The henpecked husband made an early appearance too. Asked if he had plenty of ozone in Brighton, he replies: 'Er, well – you see I had the missus with me!' Many variations appeared later.

In the beginning there were not many seaside cards but a steady market existed for Christmas, birthday and valentine cards. As the postcard trade was well established on the continent some of McGill's cards were printed in Holland or Germany. One printed in Saxony in the 'Dutch Kids' series shows a guilty looking Dutch boy with his pantaloons obviously full of apples saying, 'No, Fader – I haf no apples taken.' It is notable for the verse written by the sender on the back which reads:

> *In days of old*
> *Our Hannah bold*
> *Had promised the girls some apples.*
> *So one dark night, when the stars shone bright*
> *She managed to fill her skirt allright*
> *But her father's eyes were as good as new*
> *And he caught sight of our Hannah as she passed*
>   *through*
> *With what result, (she knew).*

This is a far cry from the more usual message,

'Wish you were here' and occasional, 'Wish you was here'. It obviously related to a personal event and I'm sure the recipient, Mrs Ward of 91 Baltic Road, Altercliffe, understood all of its nuances.

The cards printed abroad often had no border, the background was completely coloured in. Green and pink seem to have been the favourite colours. In one card a donkey boy whips one of his charges along, to the discomfort of both the beast and his boatered rider. There is space left in the caption for the sender to fill in a place name so that it reads, 'I saw an ass like this at _____. Was it you?' Later place names were overprinted on the design to increase local sales — a clever commercial idea originated by Martin Anderson the founder of the Cynicus Publishing Company. There were many 'donkey' cards to follow. The obvious pun between the careering ass and the elevated bottom of the inexperienced riders being repeated in various forms, 'Having a wonderful time here — beating all the records,' says the robust lady to her steed, and 'Don't mix with those who have too much "bounce". Take it easy!' One of the most original cards produced was not in colour at all. It was printed in black and white and shows a tethered donkey with a stable lad peering at his tail which is made of brown wool. This goes through the card in the appropriate place and is stuck at the back. It is called the 'Donkey Barometer' (to be hung in the open). The directions clearly relate the state of the tail to the weather. 'If tail dry . . . fine' 'If tail wet . . . rain' If moving, windy; moving quickly, stormy; invisible, fog; frozen, cold; and if it falls off it predicts an earthquake! The sender of the 'Barometer' in my possession wished to be anonymous but he or she had a sense of humour. The card is inscribed in a rather striking hand, 'Ye first days of Aprille!!!' It was posted in 1906. Another enquires, 'Dear Staff, How do you like this for a weather glass?'. Cards, particularly those from Germany at this time, were often decorated with tinsel and stuck with pieces of silk but this simple woollen tailed donkey proved to be so popular as a novelty that 'Copyright – Entered at Stationers Hall' was printed on the back, as a stern warning to imitators.

Despite the success of McGill's comic cards, popular cards of reigning stage beauties, view cards and novelty cards printed by the Pictorial Postcard Company, its demise came all too quickly. In 1908 Mr Percy Hutson, commonly known as Hudson, who had been a representative of the company, took over with his brother. McGill continued to work for them until 1910 and they produced a red and black series. The 'Mary had a Little Lamb' card, poorly printed and with no acknowledged publisher, was quite probably one of these. When one considers this card, dated 1909, and the black and white card showing two tramps on an LCC bench who are complaining of the Soap Trust, published the same year, during the period considered by collectors to be the Golden Age of Postcards (1900-18), then McGill was not always well served by the Hutson brothers, and there were differences in outlook. Many postcards of this period are fine examples of co-operation between artist, publisher and printer. 'Mary', in red, with the outdated bustle looks crude by comparison with photographs, often hand-coloured, of famous beauties of the theatre and music hall that were popular at the time. One of Miss Gabrielle Ray shows a saucy ankle on a card published by Wrench Ltd in 1905. 'Sorry I shan't be able to come tonight' is the message – not posted until 6.45 pm! 'Thanks for the pretty and dainty card – one of the prettiest I had,' says Amelia, following up with a coloured photo of Miss Olive May in 1910, beautifully attired and looking soulfully from card No. 229 in Misch & Stock's 'Famous Beauties' series.

McGill made no claims for his cards on aesthetic grounds. They cannot be compared for instance with the beautiful Art Nouveau cards of Alphonse Mucha – or the French salon cards of Raphael Kirchner. From the start, McGill's major aim was to amuse. His stock characters, Scotsmen, spinsters, inebriates, parlourmaids, flirts and hen-pecked husbands begin to appear in these early years, with the artist still struggling to find a consistent style. An early Jewish joke appeared dated 1908: 'I offers yer de 'and of friendship and if you've got anything you don't want I can do with it.' Remembering that Max Honnest-Reddlich and Joseph Ascher, who was to become McGill's major publisher, were German Jews, it is not surprising that only a few were published, and none at all after 1914 when Ascher was interned. One postmarked 1912 has Rub offering Solly a cigar to be greeted by the wary response 'Vat's der matter vid it?'

Certain characters were considered by McGill to be fair game but with a mother like Rosina he seldom made fun of old people. 'Can you give me something to help the Old Ladies' Home?' says the woman on the doorstep with her collecting box. 'Help 'em home? Why what have they been up to?' says the jovial resident. *(Plate 11)* Scotsmen on the other hand McGill always maintained that he belonged to a race ready to laugh at itself. From the outset there were skits on the mysteries of what might lie beneath the kilt, its propensity to reveal all in gusts of wind, and the traditional reputation of the Scot for being canny. The jokes are mild at first as in a card printed in Holland in 1912 in the Scotch Kiddies series. It reflects the pre-war use of Scotch plaid in high fashion and for children's clothes. Another from Holland that same year, makes fun of the proverbial bagpipes as a donkey's bray is mistaken by a piper for an echo. Later the jokes become more witty and then more daring, 'They made me pay in advance because I had no bags,' says the kilted Scotch visitor to the Royal Hotel in 1914. By 1916 a donkey lifts the kilt of a Scotch soldier as an officer appears. Mistaking it for a gesture from the innocent girl nearby, he mutters, 'Leave off, lassie, d'nna ye see here's the colonel comin'!!' This is another well drawn card. Attention is directed to the face of the main subject of the joke but when one looks at the detail, the colonel in miniature is drawn well and in the right proportion for the size of card. (*Plate 24*)

If the jokes were good, many cards were re-drawn. One which was printed in the States for Bamforth's 'Prohibition Series' of comics also appears in the Inter-Art Comique series. A bearded old gent in top hat and pince-nez asks Jock how the world is treating him. 'Varra seldom sir, varra seldom.' *(Plate 16)* Inter-Art Comique series. A bearded old gent in top hat and pince-nez asks Jock how the world is treating him. 'Varra seldom sir, varra seldom.' (*Plate 25*) Meanness still prevails and by 1916 the Scotsman says to the smart girl proffering the Red Cross box, 'I'm sorry Missie — I'd like fine to give you a contribution but I hae naething on me less than a penny.' This was one of Inter-Arts 'Thistle' series and bears the distinctive thistle border. The 1927 Scottish joke about Father ordering 'a cup o' tea an' four saucers' for his brood has seen many variations, being updated by other artists to a bottle of lemonade, which was later Coca Cola and four straws. It was followed by one Scot saying triumphantly to another

– 'I took Maggie 'oot last night an' I spent a poond
– she hadna' got any more!'

For anyone of my 1922 vintage who can remember the sharp sting of that cure-all iodine when splashed on an open wound, I think the best Scottish joke was made by the chubby kneed Scot who says: – 'Yer wee bairn has spilled some iodine on his hand – but it's no' wasted. I made him cut his finger!'

McGill's variations on the old Scottish jokes remained firm favourites into the sixties. People were still buying copies of the card with the clever innuendo hinted at by two ducks looking for a tasty morsel up the kilt of a sleeping Scot: 'There you are, what did I tell you?' *Plate 21.*

Some of the early spinster cards show the longing ladies as ugly witch-like creatures with long painted chins and noses. The stereotype died slowly – witness the grim creature reaching for a burglar who is dialling 999 in alarm. *(Plate 26).* This card was produced for the New McGill Comics in the 1950's. A large Amazonian woman in a 1920 card, who had captured her man and is holding him round the neck in a vice-like grip, has ugly buck teeth and yells,

58

I have caught a man at last, shout hip hip hooray!
Run and fetch a parson quick before he gets away!!

McGill exploited the idea of a husband being the answer to a maiden's prayer. Several versions of 'The shortest prayer – A man, Amen' proved popular. *(Plate 25)* Comparing earlier and later cards is interesting because they show how the limits of permissiveness were gradually extended. The earlier one shows a snub-nosed spinster kneeling by the bed, enveloped in red flannel, curlers in, eyes screwed up tightly. The inset reads:

Bless Father, Mother, Brother Bill,
Jane and Sister Liz,
But bless Oh! Bless
Beyond them all
The man who'll call me his!!

This is quite a passive spinster role if we compare it to a much later card *(Plate 17)* showing a very plump, pink lady in a petticoat, arms and knees brazenly showing, hands clasped between pendulous breasts. She eyes a picture of a he-man on the bedroom wall and says.

Please send a man to share my lot
No one knows what a lot I've got.
Rich or poor he'll still be blessed
Send him along I'll do the rest!

As women became more independent, and after two World Wars, a companion card appeared reversing the roles and showing a man in patched striped pyjamas kneeling before a pin-up girl and asking for a woman to share his lot. *(Plate 18)*

The Greetings Cards

The cards for which McGill is most remembered – the seaside ones – did not dominate the early years. There was a steady market for greetings cards to mark birthdays, St Valentine's Day, Christmas and the New Year, though in the first years of the century many people scribbled greetings on the back of any postcard which took their fancy. The elaborately decorated Christmas and valentine cards with paper, lace, ribbon, tinsel and flamboyantly embossed motifs were protected by their envelopes and subject to full letter rate of postage. For those who could not afford such luxuries the picture postcard sufficed. Birthday cards continued in this format until the thirties. The pictures on Christmas cards were not always seasonal. Often local view cards were overprinted with a Christmas or birthday message by some zealous local printer but gradually the folded Christmas card with its own envelope was widely used. However, I noticed single postcards on sale again for Christmas 1982. No doubt the cost of envelopes and the high postage, particularly the overseas rate made these cards a 'new' and attractive proposition. Their forerunners can be seen in 'A Jolly Xmas to you', 1916 version when the Government tried to stop 'treating' in pubs, and two cards in the Comique series over-printed with Christmas greetings in gold.

McGill's early style changes and fluctuates. There is a decidedly unromantic valentine card printed in Holland showing a butcher about to carve a heart and on another a skinny looking old maid who is kneeling before a check pair of trousers (and murmuring a parody on a popular ballad). Below, the message runs, 'As pants the hart for cooling stream, I hear you sigh and pine. For a good fat man to fill up these, And be your VALENTINE.' The sender had no wish for anonymity and matches the verse and the wish expressed by McGill 'May St Valentine send him along,' by her own verse: 'Come and be my Valentine/And sing me a little ditty/For in these pantaloons/You look a little dicky/Where is my wondering boy tonight?/The boy I would love with care/The boy that would be my only pride/In spite of his carroty hair.'

Unfortunately, such original outpourings on the backs of cards are rare and the writer adds, as if surprised at her daring – 'Now don't blame me for this'. The card has the typical 'Saxony' colours of pink and green, but later other valentines printed in Saxony in 1914 for Joseph Ascher have a be-ribboned blue border and a more romantic message. *(See Plates 27/28)*. One notices the high starched collar of the man sitting at his desk and the cutaway 1914 neckline, split skirt and blue hair band on the smart young lady being offered a tray of steaming hearts, no doubt representing the heat of passion from 'Toopie'. The cards are the most appropriate when the joke is relevant. One card *(Plate 23)* posted in 1907 shows a motor car leaving an astonished and battered walker man sitting at his desk and the cutaway 1914 neckline, split skirt and blue hair band on the smart young lady being offered a tray of steaming hearts, no doubt representing the heat of passion from 'Toopie'. The cards are the most appropriate when the joke is relevant. One card *(Plate 38)* posted in 1907 shows a motor car leaving an astonished and battered walker knocked down in the road, with the caption – 'A bright and happy birthday and may things come your way'. In the same series a judge sentences a man to '12 months' – 'With best wishes for the coming year – Birthday Greetings'. The face of the accused is crude but the face of the judge is masterly. *(Plate 40)* One later card plays up the grotesque quality of the 'happy, smiling faces to greet you on your birthday'. Missing teeth were not such a rarity in 1907! Only the smiles save this gruesome group. Later, as the market expanded, cards were more attractively drawn – set off on a white background with more detail in the design and the greeting. See the drawing of the typical wicker rocking chair of 1912 and the smart young lady with the fashionable blue bandeau writing her card in *Plate 39*. It is an example of McGill's drawing at its best. Compare it with some of the previous cards referred to. The differences in style can be clearly seen and were to continue throughout the early years.

3
The Early Years

In addition to the perennial appeal of the greetings cards, McGill's designs showing animals or children proved to be very popular. Babies and tots were often presented as angelic cherubs. In the first decade of the century, cards from Germany, France and Italy showed clusters of babies and young children, in various stages of undress, superimposed on trains and cars or grouped as the hearts of pansies, violets, roses — even cabbages. A motley collection of children of varying ages grace the body of an elegant, early motor car. 'A Merry Xmas' says the somewhat inappropriate legend on the back in 1905. A circle of babies' heads wreathes the mountain scene of 1906. The return of honeymooners is greeted by a field full of growing babies. They are reminded, somewhat prematurely — I think — 'One must prepare the christening as one reaps the harvest of one's love'.

America, too, had its share of artists well known for their portrayal of children. Although Kate Greenaway died in 1902 her designs of children dressed in 19th century clothing were so popular that many were printed after her death. They are still popular in the USA and are enjoying a revival here. Rose O'Neill invented 'Kewpie', a cherub with a pointed head. Ellen Clapsaddle was producing lovely cards of little charmers in delightful costumes. Bertha Corbett invented the 'sun-bonnet' babies. Nearer home, Mabel Lucie Attwell's pink, round-faced cherubic children appeared in 1911 and remained firm favourites with doting parents until the Second World War.

With so much wide-eyed innocence published it is perhaps not surprising that in 1911 the sender of McGill's alternative to the famous 'Fido' card writes to a nurse: 'Do not be too shocked with card. It beats all I have yet sent — and I've sent a few.' The kneeling child in this version is being teased by a small boy in pyjamas. 'Please, Lord, excuse me a minute while I kick Herby!' The children's nightly prayers feature in several cards. A sickly, sweet little girl kneeling by a cradle and pointing out to God that the baby's 'toofies' have been forgotten says, 'I wish you could spare time to come an' finish him!' By 1914 the sentiment expressed by a little boy, who had obviously just been belted by his disappearing dad, was somewhat stronger, 'and bless Father too — but NOT MUCH!' (This card from Ada, dated 9 January 1914, bears the tidings that one or two handkerchiefs have been sent to, 'My Dear Lovey, I only paid 1s0¾d per dozen — so don't grumble about them will you?' Not all cards yield such nostalgia and I reflect that my tissue-scattering grandchildren have never used such old fashioned accessories!) Another child's prayer card shows a little boy by his bed, hands clasped, muttering – 'An' if I die before I wake – Please excuse me coming to Heaven in my pyjamas!' Death was not a popular theme, and the card did not sell well. Another version appeared in 1920. The prayer changed to ' – an' please make me a good boy, so's Pa can't sneak out of buying me that bike.'

A popular and much more realistic card exploited the idea, seen in the Scotch card, that to a goose or gosling, the penis might resemble a tasty worm. In the 'Modern Kids' Series, No 409, printed for Ascher in Saxony and postmarked 1912, a little boy with his back to the fence protects his little willie from a hungry goose. 'Oh Lord, if ever you wants to show how you loves little boys what tries hard to be good – now's your time!!' McGill's jokes centring on the penis are not as overt as some of today's. They work through innuendo and euphemism. The child with a black eye who has come off worst in a fight says, 'Well I'm blowed – and I only called him Little Willie!' appeared in 1907. Many different versions of Little Willie, Johnny and Charlie appeared later.

Up to the 1920s the jokes range from the harmless – a little girl covered in paint, 'I've too much on my hands to write,' and the little boy cutting the bobbles off a blue chenille tablecloth, 'She lufs me – she lufs me not' – to the genuinely funny – as in, the bird with his worm hovering over the yelling baby in the pram, 'Dammit, take it, if it'll keep you quiet,' and the queasy tot leaving church wiping her face after being sick in the box reserved for contributions, 'For the sick' – 'It's a good job that box was there!' she sighs with relief. 'Don't soap taste nasty in your eye,' says the baby just out of the bath. Often adult sentiments and sexuality were ascribed to children, making their remarks seemingly innocent and supposedly more acceptable. 'Oh! He said Damn!' says the little girl, protecting her doll from the stubborn little boy. Another mini-virago having felled a little boy to the floor, brandishes a spade above the caption: ' – an' so I put on my hat an' I went. Though she didn't exactly say NO, I could see it was NO that she meant!'

A pre-war 'piccaninny' in a tub says, 'If cleanliness am nex' to Godliness me rather stay a lit' heathen.' It's just as well perhaps that there were very few jokes involving black children. By the end of the war the joke had progressed to, 'Cleanliness is next to Godliness but this water is as hot as ———!!' Very daring.

McGill was quite capable of drawing attractive babies and children. In the early days he had his small daughters to observe. 'I'm looking after my own affairs' says the little girl pinning up her knickers. 'And a woman's work is never done,' says the pig-tailed tot with broom and bucket. This card is perhaps one of his best child paintings *(Plate 64)*. McGill must have liked it for he sent it to himself. One wonders, when he could paint like this, why he drew at the same time so many children with large heads out of all proportion to their bodies. Since he concentrated on the facial expressions of the adults he may have felt it necessary to stress the child's head. *See* the curly headed baby bloated on his bottle 'The Curse of Drink'. The device did not deter buyers so it must have fallen within the current canon of 'cuteness'.

Not writing was used as a constant theme. The draughtsman's hand can be see in *Plate 49* an early card produced for the Woolstone brothers. This was followed by one suitably illustrated and printed for Joseph Ascher in 1913. 'It's a long time since Noah was in the Ark and it's a long time since Julius Caesar landed but it's a devil of a long time since you've written'. There was a Scottish version and, of course, the pillar box is frequently featured, as was the verse:

I was going to send a letter,
But I think a postcard's better
So I'm sending you this friendly little line
It's not so very pretty, and it's not so very witty
But it shows I don't forget you all the time.

Over seventy years after this card was posted, when visiting an old people's club recently, I repeated the first line to a group of octogenarians who immediately chipped in with the rest. There was no prompting and the lines came out as firmly as those of the nursery rhymes which linger for ever in the back of our memories. They must have made a deep impression at the time. There was a Scottish version posted on HMS Canada in February 1918, and stamped, 'Passed by the Censor'. The wee Scot says,

Though I canna greet ye
Though I canna meet ye
Yer hand to take
This little card I sen' ye
This little line I pen ye
For Auld Times Sake.

A witty pillar-box card shows a dog sitting near the box looking ruefully at the wet patch nearby, for which he's responsible – 'I'm sorry I missed the post.' *(Plate 32)*

Animal cards were often sent to children, though the joke was more than likely to be an adult one, with the animals in human situations. Ma and pa cat arriving for the holidays with a litter of kittens, refer euphemistically to the fact that 'We have all got some "little troubles" these days.' The beribboned tabby serenades the black and white Tom to the tune of 'Come, come I want you only'. One startled puss with sticking plaster displayed prominently on his rear says, 'Damn those broken bottles anyway.' A ginger tomcat sits forlorn at a closed front door — 'Well if that ain't the limit! We only get married this morning and they've forgotten to put her out for the night.'

All pretty harmless stuff. McGill's style, fluctuates between the flat cartoon and the more realistic drawing. *(Plate 36)* 'I'm coming home absolutely stoney — but am travelling with some jolly companions' — which turn out to be carefully drawn cows — was done in 1913. A consistent style was still elusive. Of course, when one thinks of animal cards, Louis Wain will always be associated with brilliantly drawn cards of almost human cats, George Studdy with the white and black spotted dog Bonzo, Otto Mesmer and Pat Sullivan with Felix the cat who kept on walking, Lawson Wood with the wise old monkey, Gran'pop, Walt Disney with Mickey Mouse and Donald Duck cards, which were printed in many countries in their thousands. Donald McGill will be remembered mainly for his fat sea-side holiday makers. Not so well-known is his brilliant series of cockerel cards. The original painting in my posession of an almost featherless cockerel retains all the pride of the barnyard rooster. He used this image for a wartime propaganda card about egg rationing during the Second World War. Surrounded by three hens the magnificent creature exhorts them to:

Gather round me little hens,
Though I'm not a beauty
If it's eggs the country wants
We ALL must do our duty.

On a lighter note there's a comment on the building boom after the First World War. One cockerel confides in another about his hen who has just laid two cubes, 'Yes, last week she got chased by a builder, an' I'm blessed if she hasn't been laying foundation stones ever since!'

Other favourites were the hen sidling up to her Cock, 'Oh Horace, I've something to tell you, I'm going to have an egg!' and the cockerel gazing at an egg saying, 'I'm getting a bit suspicious after something my wife let drop last night!' Of course the stork was also always a good subject for a joke.

There was an early 'Funny Parrot' series printed in Saxony. One shows a parrot swearing and a cat round the corner comments, 'Hullo, I thought Master was out.' By 1920 this joke had been enlarged *(see Plate 33)* to show a young lady saying, 'Why should I want a husband? I've got a parrot that swears, a dog that growls, a lamp that smokes – and a cat that stops out all night!' There were plenty of cards featuring the seaside donkeys which McGill must have observed during the family holidays on Hayling Island, and there were some interesting studies of racehorses which illustrated jokes about the inveterate racegoer, who, sporting top hat, binoculars, spats and loud check suit always lost his money. He says, 'I backed a horse at 20 to 1 and it didn't come in till half past two . . .' His working class counterpart was drawn in flat cap, with a jug of beer, clutching the Racing Special while the horses gallop across a frieze on top of the card. 'I had ten bob on each way,' says his bowlered companion 'but I didn't know the bloomin' 'orse was going to run backwards.' An old joke, but betting as a form of escapism appears to have loomed large on the working man's horizon pre-dating today's legendary win on the Pools. There is an oblique reference to the *Sporting Times* which was published continuously from 1865 to 1930. It gave all the racing news and was popularly known as 'The Pink 'Un'. *Plate 39* is unusual with its pink border. McGill uses the term 'The Pink 'Un' though the joke concerns a red-nosed gentleman chatting up the barmaid. One was sent to a barmaid at the Crown & Sceptre in 1908. The sender improved on McGill's, 'It's very strange but I really can't remember whether I promised the wife to drink two whiskies and be home at ten, or to have ten drinks and be in bed by two!' by adding 'or to kiss the barmaid twice.' The frequency and speed of the post in those days can be gathered by the message posted at 9.30 am asking Dora 'to *write* and let me know if I may call for you tomorrow Friday, about two —'.

Pert and pretty barmaids feature often in McGill cards *(Plate 40)* and they are always more than a match for the mashers or 'knuts' — gentlemen of leisure who fancied themselves as lady-killers. 'Don't swank about mashing the barmaids' say the girls, 'They're not smiling at you they're laughing at you.' The girl staying in Dyserth in 1912 claims that's 'where the knuts come from.' She has christened the monocled young Romeo 'Glad-Eye Joe' and states, after the popular song, 'He was standing at the corner of the street'. The mashers appear less frequently after this. No doubt the war diminished their numbers. The slum dweller and the hen-pecked working class husband gradually replace him. An early card of the unshaven husband in his night shirt coping with two screaming babies appeared in 1908, heralding a long line of brow-beaten men. 'Happy Returns' it says on the back. There may have been suffragette overtones to this card. By 1920 hubby is coping with a screaming baby and cooking his supper on a paraffin stove, at the same time, 'I'd have written before if I hadn't had such a lot on my hands'. *(Plate 34)*

Donald McGill laid no claim to being any kind of social historian but, as his postcards covered a period of nearly six decades, tantalising glimpses of the times are inevitably, though probably unconsciously displayed. There were few political references since the topical card dates rapidly. He supported Lloyd George's social measures. His daughter remembers him quickly sketching Lloyd George as the Conservatives saw him – a devil – then as the Liberals saw him – an angel – and, with a few lightning strokes, Lloyd George as he really was. One of his best puns is used on a card of an empty cradle published for Joseph Ascher after Lloyd George's government brought in legislation for Maternity Benefit which became available by July 1912.

> *There's no need be short of money*
> *Or for joining the 'great unemployed'*

Just fill this and you get thirty shillings
By GEORGE! It is a joy una-Lloyd.

We can see how time changes the acceptable boundaries of humour. By 1927 the same empty cradle rocks beneath the bold statement 'We have nothing to put in it but we're doing our best' – and for once there is no exclamation mark. Ena and Syd divulge the news that they are having a scrumptious time at Lowestoft and 'we are having one of the opposite sides (a cradle) made to order.' Reading between the lines it is obvious that the fears and prejudices of the 19th century purists about the openness of the postcard's message had long been overcome.

The job of the comic postcard artist was to make people laugh, not to moralise. The railway networks disgorged their 'trippers' at the seaside resorts by the thousand, all set for a Bacchanalian break. Charles Booth and Henry Mayhew had exposed the appalling living conditions of the poor in London in the 19th century. Conditions in the industrial cities like Manchester, Liverpool and the mill towns were still grim in the 20th century. When factories closed for the 'Wakes' week, determined holidaymakers left behind slum tenements, appalling sanitation and deficiency diseases like tuberculosis.

A 1909 advertisement recommends Harrison's Nursery Pomade to kill nits and vermin. Soap was an expensive item in the household budget. Toilet soap was beyond the reach of most workers who had to budget for Lifebuoy — 3 bars for 8½d (3½p), or Carbolic sold by weight at 7 lb for 2/- (10p). Carbolic powder was advertised to destroy bad odours and prevent fever. With British doggedness the working class holidaymaker endured crowded 'trip trains', bulging boarding houses, inferior food, fleas, lice and bed-bugs. The attention of the latter was the subject of many a joke. 'Ah've got something up my sleeve,' says the Scot scratching his arm. The small boy tugging at his collar asks for a 'Penn'orth o' Insec Powder please, an' put it right down here!' 'Come down here before they get full up' says the caption above a drawing of a boarder sleeping on each stair. Hotels were for the well-to-do, boarding houses and lodgings for the workers. 'We came down by a cheap train,' says the lady hiding two children under her skirt and asking for one ticket. 'Hurry up and come,' says the man travelling on the coal tender. *(Plate 35)*.

Sea-sickness was another hazard for the town dweller on the *Skylark*. The determination of the tripper to enjoy the welcome break from routine has to be admired. Mary writes from Blackpool: 'No more Isle of Man for me I was sick each way, but it has done me good!' McGill rarely lapsed into bad taste but the reference to the sinking of the Titanic by the sick passenger, 'I've got no luck — *We* shall never run into any iceberg' does him little credit. More in his style, is the picture of a sea-sick passenger, hand raised against the approach of a rotund sailor. 'I can stand nearly anything — but keep fat away from me.' Richard Carline writing in *Pictures in the Post* points out that the editor of the *Picture Postcard Magazine*, in February 1903, declared that sea-sickness is 'A very unpleasant subject and one, in our opinion utterly unfit for portraying on a postcard.' The subject however still made lesser mortals laugh. 'Cheer up young man' says the jolly matron to the sea-sick 'Sunday' sailor 'I've brought up a family of ten children.' This interplay of caption and picture shows McGill at his best. In another card a bowler hatted sandwich-board man says 'I've got a good job here, so much a day and my board.'

A well-drawn card shows the masher being seduced away from Prof. Maggit's improving lecture on 'Wire Worms in Wurzels' by a smart young lady dressed to kill in pre-war fashion. The postcard has been over-printed 'Ramsgate'. The sender in elegant hand reveals something of the atmosphere in a visit to neighbouring Margate in 1913. 'I hear you are all having a ripping time of it,

I sometimes feel I should like to be one with you but the sleep accommodation is right off. You know how one poor chap had to be put on the shelf? This is a glorious day to be at the sea-side — altho' only a tripper. Margate is very full I never saw such a crowd everywhere — and the dresses, Well! — What little I saw quite confounded me!' There is a hint of the feeling of being a second-class citizen in 'only a tripper' and one sighs for the writer with an undecipherable signature. As for the dresses, the fashion designers seemed determined to confound and McGill's cards reflect the changing fashions very faithfully right up to the 1940s when fashions were changing more rapidly.

The Edwardian era, 1901–1910, saw the gradual release of women from the artificial constrictions of the 'S' shape corset, idealised by the American artist Charles Dana Gibson. From 1895 one of the beautiful Langhorne sisters, Irene, who was to become his wife, was also his model. To achieve a silhouette similar to hers women forced themselves into tightly laced corsets which constricted the waist, pushed up the bust and emphasised the bottom. Camille Clifford even invented a Gibson walk — and women slavishly followed. It was the French fashion designer Paul Poiret who released women from this unnatural stance in 1908, by providing a new style straight corset which was meant to follow the natural line of the figure. It was cut with a low bustline and brassières, which were to become a mainstay of comic cards, followed later to make up the deficiency. The straight line of the corset dipped at the front, curving over the hip-line. McGill depicts it perfectly in *Plate 41* and also illustrates the novelty of the telephone. 'Oh Mother, how can I speak to him like this,' says the shy girl in her underwear.

Having released women's torsos from the 'S' bend, Paul Poiret confounds us by imprisoning the legs in the straight narrow skirt, aptly called the 'hobble' skirt. The lace frills and furbelows and the bell-shaped skirt of the early Edwardian period gave way to a more tailored look. Skirts went naughtily above the ankle, 'So far so good' and as the hem narrows the hat becomes larger so that the silhouette tapers towards the feet. Some of the cards up to 1911 and 1912 give a very good impression of the evolution in fashion. Hats became so ridiculously large that advice to men about to marry, shows a man practising holding an umbrella over an outsize hat which he is wheeling on a trolley. Dresses were fastened with numerous tiny, matching buttons so that papa was in great demand when mama was dressing. 'Mother when you've finished with Father, I should like to borrow him for a minute!' says the little girl trying to tie the draw-string in her knickers. You may wonder how it is that Donald McGill mirrors the fashions so faithfully. His daughter believes it was because her mother had a flair for dressmaking. She made all her own and the children's clothes, copying the fashion plates of the time. Grandmother Hurley had always been up-to-date and Florence and her two sisters had had the use of the sewing room at the Music Hall. McGill's accessories are always right for their time too. He transfers the hobble skirted ladies to the seaside in a series of Saxony cards called 'Sea-side Art' *(Plate 37)* and later puts them into the daring one piece swim suits, that end at mid thigh, 'Legs and shoulders are cheap today,' says the butcher's boy looking on. *(Plate 38)*

By 1905 skirts, blouses and pleated tailored suits, even knickerbockers, which could cope better with the demands of new activities like bicycling, were establishing themselves. At the same time the suffragettes were agitating for women's emancipation and it is difficult to understand how the restrictive hobble skirt was so slavishly followed in 1910. It was influenced by a combination of Paul Poiret's designs and the effect of the explosion of colour and orientalism used in the designs of Leon Bakst for the Russian Ballet *Scheherezade* which was performed in London that year. Bold, bright, oriental colours – purple, shocking pink, apple green – replaced the washed out pastels of the late Victorian and early Edwardian period. In order to emulate the slave-girls of the oriental harem, the boldest amongst the fashion-conscious took to wearing pantaloon trousers which showed beneath a matching three-quarter length coat. This outfit was known as the 'Harem Skirt'. Its popularity was short-lived as it was greeted with howls of derision. There was some anxiety shown by hardened chauvinists; it took a war to tolerate women in trousers. At this stage, 1911–12, a policeman is shown holding back the crowd when the wind reveals the Harem skirt:

Mary had a little skirt and it was all the go
But Mary had to call a cab, when the stormy winds
* did blow.*

'Any braces today, Lady?' taunts the pedlar to the astonished lady in pink. The working class version shows Auntie who has borrowed her husband's trousers. 'Auntie *will* be in the fashion' comments McGill. By 1913 the high collar was being abandoned, it was the 'V' neck of the 'pneumonia' blouse which was causing a sensation and, as dyeing processes improved, synthetic furs and fur trimming became the rage. 'Have you any skunk?' asks the lady in the store. 'Yes, Madame – see the

Boss!' replies the lady assistant, indicating a grim-faced manager with moustache and red bow tie.

McGill was faithful to male fashion too, though this changed more slowly. The Edwardian frock-coat differed little from its late Victorian counterpart and, with the top hat and spats and gloves, was considered the correct formal day wear for men of substance, up to the First World War. *(See previous plate).* Dinner suits and tails were worn in the evening and, gradually, under the influence of the Prince of Wales, the lounge suit became acceptable, together with the green velour 'Homburg' hat, which he popularised after visiting the German spa from which it took its name. McGill makes fun of the Homburg showing it rammed down on the head, providing cover for the man who has got the missus down with him. In making fun of the latest fashion craze, McGill was following in the footsteps as such satirists as Hogarth, Rowlandson, Cruickshank and Robert Seymour, who illustrated part of the Pickwick Papers. Seymour's broadsheet shown was produced in the early 1830's — and the sentiment 'Delicacy — Lawk's Fred, it's not fashionable, beside's, wot's the good o' having a fine leg if one mustn't show it!' was the precursor to many a McGill joke.

The summer straw boater, the soft trilby hat and the bowler persist throughout the period along with bow ties, waistcoats, gloves, high starched collars. The narrow trousers and velvet faced jackets of Edwardian times were copied in the 1950s by the 'Teddy' boys who fancied themselves, as the 'mashers' had done before them.

By the outbreak of war in 1914 – McGill knew those areas of humour which were most likely to tickle the fancy of the common man. There were children whose comments by the 1920s became more precocious – 'Mummie is Aunt Jane a blood relation?' 'Yes dear.' 'Mummie is she the bloodiest relation we have?' *(Plate 59).* The 1912 courting couple – 'Shall we take a long tramp across country tomorrow?' 'Take him if you like of course, but I'd just as soon, we went alone!' answers the gentleman in evening dress. Honeymooners, of course, were always good for a laugh. Inebriation and the deterioration of wedded bliss had popular appeal. The skinny wife admonishes her overweight drunken husband in a card printed in Holland as early as 1910, 'You wretch, if you come home drunk again I'll never speak to you any more!' 'Thatsh it, M'ma puttin' temptation in my way!!' The henpecked husband and the plight of the spinster caused their fair share of mirth. The double entendre was well established. The country girl kissing her boyfriend says, 'Doctor says I should take it regular,' and the young soldier courting the nurse-maid by the pram

83

says, 'I don't know what you mean, what about the baby?' Malapropisms diminish as the public becomes better educated but cards hinting at bodily functions, obesity, the sheer enjoyment of the seaside and the annual release from long hours of drudgery and routine work found a ready market.

There were many jokes relating flatulence to sea breezes – 'It's very windy but I'm enjoying myself at Weston-super-Mare.'

'The longer we stay the more we like it' say the couple clasping hands as they paddle. (1912) 'We're always merry and bright.' (1913) 'It's just the place for us young folk,' gasps a big bottomed girl as she smacks the water. It was printed for Joseph Ascher in Bavaria in 1914 and together with 'I'm having a fine blow', posted that July, these cards express all the innocent enjoyment of a world not yet at war *(Plates 74-76).*

4
1914-1930

With one foot amputated Donald McGill was not eligible to join the armed forces during the 1914 – 18 war, in any case, he was by then 39. As he showed no trace of a limp and looked young for his age, he had to face considerable pressure and ignorant enquiries about the fact that he was not serving in France. Lord Kitchener's recruiting poster with its accusing finger was pointing from every hoarding with the exhortation that your King and Country needed you. Coming from a family with a strong military tradition, McGill coped with his own disappointment as philosophically as possible. During the war he worked very hard, turning out an average of nine cards a week.

The Admiralty declared itself in favour of certain cards being sent to the troops, recognising their role as morale boosters. Quite early in the war, cards had to be submitted to the scrutiny of the censor. Such slogans as 'British Made' and 'British Manufacture Throughout' began to appear on postcards. This was obviously considered politic when one remembers the former reliance of the industry on Germany. Later, the recipients were urged to 'Buy

85

National War Bonds Now'. Of course, this was not the first time that postcards had been used as propaganda or morale boosters. Apart from the small light-weight cards dropped by balloon during the Paris siege of 1870, soldiers on both sides were served by what are often claimed to be the first picture postcards. In 1870, Mr Schwartz, a German stationer produced cards for German soldiers with drawings of a German artillery man and the battlefield. In 1871, Mr Leon Bernardeaux, a French stationer, sold cards for the Breton troops stationed at Conlie to send back to their families. Cards were also produced during the Boer War (1899–1902). Whilst the London-born American Caton-Woodville, Harry Payne and Lance Thackeray were busy producing cards to whip up public enthusiasm and the British soldiers' morale, cards ridiculing the British stance and favouring the South African leader, Kruger, were being produced in France and Germany. In the First World War German cards were as patriotic and sentimental as the British and French ones, but humour was not their strong line.

An old sweat – 'Old Bill' – a Tommy drawn by Bruce Bairnsfather began to appear on postcards which were immediately popular. They were based on his own experience and struck a humorous and, at the same time, a realistic note. Even more realistic were the sets of cards, eight for 6d (2½p), printed from battle photographs taken for the *Daily Mail*. They appeared in August 1916 and even the *Mail* was staggered by the response. Millions of cards were printed — a record of the appalling conditions, the traumas of trench warfare and the incredible fortitude and gallantry of those who served in France. At the same time human sentiment, the yearning of lovers, wives and families to be together again was expressed through cards showing photographs, often hand-coloured, of soldiers and sailors dreaming of home. Songs like 'I hear you calling me' and 'Love that will not let me go' touched the heart strings and no doubt were indicative of sentiments truly expressed by the sender, but the soldiers' sense of humour would not be suppressed even in the trenches and many of the first patriotic and sentimental songs were parodied.

First hand experience of the war was denied to Donald McGill and sentiment he catered for by dressing up his 'Cute Kiddies' in uniform. The two cards reproduced are the only examples known to me of privately commissioned work carried out by McGill. They were drawn by him to the designs of the late Captain A.C. Fawssett, DSO of HMS *Achilles* in the 1914-18 war and so far enshrine quite a number of unanswered questions. They were produced from originals in the possession of Mrs

Ann Atkin, of the Gnome Reserve, in Devon. She is Captain Fawssett's daughter and these originals are kept in a frame labelled on the back in the Captain's handwriting: 'Picture postcards designed by myself, drawn by Donald McGill. Published and sold to the Officers and Ships Coy of HMS *Achilles* during the war of 1914-18.' So far as I know, they are the only originals dating from this period and are well preserved though there is some fading of the yellows on one.

The main questions lie in the subject and contents. The figure of both male and female are typically McGill, being his cute or repulsive children according to your taste, but the total symbolism, most particularly of the very oddly shaped helmets, has not been clarified despite much enquiry. According to Mrs Atkin, Captain Fawssett was indeed in command and if this is so, he was not much over 30 years of age at the time. Could they have possibly met or did the Captain simply get in touch with Inter Art Co. and its proprietor Robert McCrum so that the just commissioned Donald to produce the work as outlined? The apparent French allusion in the colouring of the pennants, could quite reasonably be the signal 'Line Ahead' — but oh! those helmets! Surely the discipline of the navy does not allow for a naughty joke based on a highly distorted version of a battle helmet?

One wonders about McGill's personal feelings when he drew the child in soldier's uniform with the caption, 'Brings the war home to you doesn't it − all of us military chaps about!', or the well drawn illustration of the popular song, 'Goodbye-ee-'. *(Plate 46)* However, he made a good joke about the farmer who wasn't at the front.

With five million dead on the allied side alone by 1918, the McGill card sent just a few days before the war started, with a picture of a man enjoying his 1/6d pint and the caption, 'It's better to be alive with 18 pence than dead with a thousand pounds,' sounded an unconsciously prophetic note. As a comic card artist it was not McGill's job to philosophise about the war but to lighten the load with a laugh. He adapted his birthday cards in a 'Birthday Tommy' series and in 1915 a 'Recruits' series appeared with a patriotic red, white and blue border showing the new recruit faced with the daily fatigue duties. A Tommy sweating under a sack of coal from Kitchener's Recruits' coal store says, 'Well I've done my bit if I never see a German.' Surprisingly, the concentration on the domestic trials of the soldiers' life was very popular. Perhaps it made an abnormal situation seem normal. There were jokes about the weight of kit when carried in full marching orders, 'The flipping fleas' the ill-fitting uniforms, − 'the trousers are a bit tight under the arm-pits!!' The sergeant major's raucous yell was called 'The voice that breathed o'er Eden.' Orders of the day state '8 hours drill, 8 hours route march, 8 hours trenching − God Save the King,' and the recruit mutters, ' − and then we have the rest of the day to ourselves.' The private, sweltering as he carries large dixies full of hot soup from the field kitchen, and the allotment holder trying to ease the food shortages, have to face the question, 'Daddy what did you do in the Great War?' There is underlying anxiety expressed even though a card is illustrated by a washing line full of bloomers, 'Do send a line as to your whereabouts.' The Scots lass sends a card to her kilted soldier, 'To greet ye, though I canna meet ye, I'm to your memory true.' The smart young lady in 1915 is shown writing, 'Lest you forget I'm still alive/This card I send today/So drop a line with all the news/Since I have been away.'

There are poignant messages scribbled on the back of cards from France − 'We're moving on tonight − I sent you a card last night, but as things are I think it best to send another this morning.' There are some light-hearted courting cards. 'No games are allowed to be played on this common' says the notice. 'We'd better go further on George,' says the soldier's girl. The idea was used again in 1920 with the couple now in civvies of course. The card with the soldier and his girl on a bench in the moonlight has English and French captions 'I'm having a fine time here, but the best part of the day is the night!' There are puns, of course – 'Another big draught going to the front!' says the rotund soldier, draining his outsize tankard – and euphemisms, 'Germans retreat cut off' says the Daily Snail. 'Well, I don't suppose it hurt 'im any more than some of the wounds our poor fellers get.'

Other aspects of the war are treated with the lightest touch and civilians and servicemen alike could not get enough of McGill's cards. 'Mines in the North Sea' reads the little girl clutching her sailor boy's photo – 'So's mine'. The special constable asks the red-nosed drunk to put his light out. The shocked lady who wants to do her bit in the munitions factory draws the line at working 'in shifts'. There was a series of cards about rationing which was introduced in the spring of 1918. Food hoarders were denounced and prosecuted. The traditionally jovial fat man was temporarily out of favour. 'Eat slowly, and you will need less food,' said the posters. 'No shortage of fats down here' says the McGill card with four portly bathers. 'We will now form a committee to sit on the supply of eggs,' says the vicar to the astonished lady churchgoers. Belts were tightened, 'It's a struggle to make ends meet' says the beach baby biting his toe. In the cold winter of 1917, coal was rationed and 'Keep the home fires burning' may have had a hollow ring. Before 'The End in Sight' – a German soldier's rear punctured by a Tommy's bayonet – 'our boys' appear on the cards – still courting and cheeky – but in hospital blue.

The 'Peace at Last' theme was humorously treated with the widower of Martha Nagg resting smug and self-satisfied on his wife's grave-stone and later a companion card showing Mrs Naggitt standing unrepentant by her husband's grave-stone. Both cards were issued with French captions: 'Enfin La Paix', 'Repose en paix – jusqu'au jour au nous nous retrouverons.' *(Plate 60)*

From the war years through to the late 1920s McGill produced what I consider to be his best work. The cards are well balanced and composed and, considering the printing limitations, the colour renderings are subtle. *(See Plate 62 'The Last Post', 'La Denière étape', sent from a field post office in 1918).* Before the soldiers went 'over the top', many to face death, the trenches and the ground nearby would be scattered with risqué French postcards which they did not want to be found on their person. Homely comic cards drawn by McGill were found still tucked in pockets and wallets – evidence of a young man's innocence.

At home, dogged fortitude marked the closing

years of the war and a certain amount of industrial unrest which was to lead to the General Strike of 1926. 'I aint no spouter my proper place is on the scaffold,' says the builder's mate and this may have reflected the mood of some. By the end of the war, wounded Indian soldiers were convalescing in the Pavilion at Brighton and some of the austerity measures were easing off — the time had come at last to 'pack up your troubles'. There was what with hindsight looks like a desperate gaiety.

Steam is superseded
Electricity is King;
The 40 horse power motor
Is quite the proper thing —

Progress is our motto
New things have come to stay
But thank heavens we still have Babies,
In the good old fashioned way!

New fangled electric light spread out on the grid system in 1926. 'Why don't you blow the light out, Jarge?' says the newly-wed. 'I can't — it's in a bottle!' Gramophones ground out ragtime. 'Don't care, I've learnt to jazz' says the battered boy with a black eye. 'Everybody's doing it, why shouldn't we?' say the courting couple naughtily. Two jolly ladies in calf-length skirts and dashing 'V' necklines prance gaily along, 'You bet there'd be a "Hot Time in the old town to-night" — if I were with you!!' 'It must be awful for a woman to be tempted!' 'It's far worse not to be!' quips the Eton-cropped girl showing her green garters.

Necklines and waistlines dropped as skirts got shorter and heels higher. The boyish, flattened figures in the straight chemise dresses had gone to the other extreme from Camille Clifford's 'S' bend. By 1927 the hem line audaciously reached just above the knee. The new short hair style fitted snugly under tight-fitting cloche hats or was set off by coloured bandeaux spanning the forehead. Flesh coloured stockings began to appear. Bangles and beads drew attention to exposed arms and necks. Once again there were protests from the pulpit and from Mr and Mrs Grundy. James Laver in his book *Costume and Fashion — a concise history* points out that the Archbishop of Naples declared the Amalfi earthquake 'was due to the anger of God against a skirt which reached no further than the knee.'! He also quotes the example of two American states which tried to legislate to promote their own view of morality — Utah, where a fine and imprisonment were threatened for those who wore 'skirts higher than three inches above the ankle,' and Ohio which sought to prohibit any female over 14 years of age

94

from wearing a skirt 'which does not reach that part of the foot known as the instep.' Attempts to restrain fashion within a corset of legislation have never been very successful. The freedom of the 1920s fashions had been accelerated by the new found independence of women at war and was an absolute gift to McGill. The wide necklines of the new evening gowns led to many jokes about undressing to be 'fully dressed'. The dark tail coat and matching trousers, stiff collar, white bow tie and starched dress shirt was still being worn by the man about town in the evenings. He sported black patent shoes, top hat, white gloves, opera cloak and silver-topped stick. These McGill faithfully reproduced, along with the black waistcoat and bow tie worn with a dinner jacket for less formal occasions. Frock coats were overtaken by lounge-suits and the new 'Oxford bags', as the wide-legged trousers of 1925 were called, inevitably became the butt of many postcard jokes.

One can follow the fashions in beachwear too – the 1920s bathing dress was midway between the all enveloping Victorian caleçons of the 1870's and the brief bikinis of the 1960's. The tide was moving fast. Compare the navy blue ASA 'regulation' swim suits, one with sleeves, worn by the five Goodacre sisters, swimming champions in 1923, with those of the late twenties – coloured, backless, striped, laced at the sides. The plump middle-aged 'bathing belle' shows off:

My new bathing dress
Is quite a success;
What you can't see of me
Of course you must guess!

To cater for the French market 'Je crois que je fais sensation!' You can see her counterpart, more exposed of course, on the beaches around Britain today. Mrs Bloggs, the sensation of Bridlington, Brighton or Bournemouth trying vainly to match fantasy with reality. The arrival of the bikini made McGill re-vamp his bathing belle. *(Plate 68)*

The fashions may change but the spirit of McGill's jokes remained. By the 1920s and 1930s it was no crime to be plump. Too many people went to bed hungry to make weight-watching a fashionable fad. Overloading the seaside weighing machines was a cause for mirth and the bumping of big backsides all part of the fun – 'We're only just making ends meet at Mablethorpe.' 'I haven't a waist any more – it's a circumference,' chuckles the fat bather at Margate. Obesity is good for a laugh again as little Willie is lost beneath the paunch of his boatered dad. Over the years the child and its parent both change sex but the joke

I'd have written before if I hadn't
such a lot on my hands!

"Why should I want a husband? I've got
a parrot that swears, a dog that growls,
a lamp that smokes—and a cat that stops
out all night!"

Come down here before they get full up.

I'M COMING HOME ABSOLUTELY STONEY

BUT AM TRAVELLING WITH SOME JOLLY COMPANIONS !

"PLENTY OF OZONE DOWN HERE, OLD MAN."
"YES, BUT NO GOOD TO ME; I'VE GOT THE MISSIS DOWN WITH ME!"

7

"LEGS & SHOULDERS ARE CHEAP TO-DAY!"

8

THINGS ARE A BIT TIGHT
BUT I'M PICKING UP
AT EASTBOURNE

"MR SMITH IS IT ? ASK HIM TO
COME TO DINNER TO-MORROW."
"OH MOTHER ! HOW CAN I SPEAK
TO HIM LIKE THIS !!"

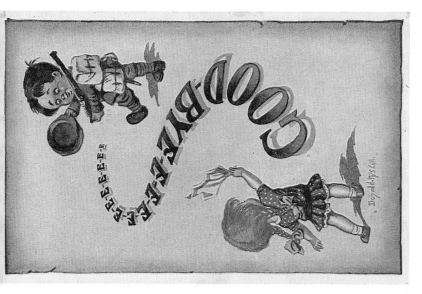

"DADDY, WHAT DID YOU DO
IN THE GREAT WAR?"

"J'espère que tu nous raconteras tes
campagnes?"

I'm having a fine time here, but the best part of the day is the night!

On dira ce qu'on voudra, le plus beau moment de la journée c'est la nuit!

"WELL, I DONT SUPPOSE IT HURT 'IM ANY MORE THAN SOME OF THE WOUNDS THAT OUR POOR FELLERS GET !!"

FORMATION D'UN GROS CONTINGENT
POUR LE FRONT.

ANOTHER BIG DRAUGHT
GOING TO THE FRONT !

IT'S BETTER
TO BE ALIVE
WITH 18
PENCE

THAN DEAD WITH
A THOUSAND
POUNDS.

£1000

WE'RE "ALWAYS MERRY AND BRIGHT"

51

MABLETHORPE.

We're only just making ends meet

52

Maudie 's 'nothing on' to-day,
Maudie dresses so.

To-morrow though she 's 'something on'
And 'fully dressed' she 'll go !!

"SHE WAS TRYING TO BE CAREFUL
HE WAS TRYING TO BE GOOD."

"I suppose you're giving him all he wants?"
"Oh, Doctor, he's been far too ill to think about anything of that sort!"

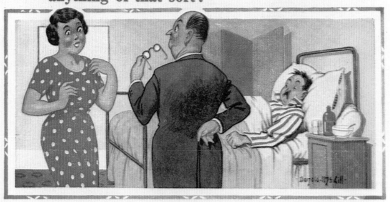

"If you were a doctor, I could show you something that would astonish you!"

" Mummie, is Aunt Jane a blood relation ? '

" Yes, dear."

" Mummie, is she the bloodiest relation we have ? "

SACRED
TO THE
MEMORY
OF
MARTHA NAGG

R.I.P.

MN.
1924.

Peace at last !

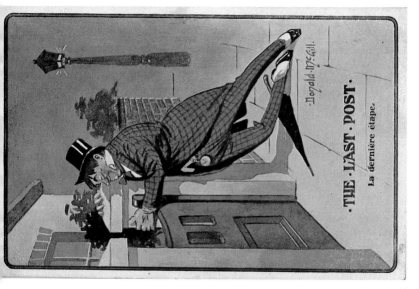

· THE · LAST · POST ·

La dernière étape.

" Why don't one of you take th'other arm ? "

remained a firm favourite until the 1960s and was copied by many other artists. The captions and the hasty messages scribbled to impress friends and neighbours show a reluctance to face the fact that the holiday must end.

The Bank Holiday Act of 1871 made sure that everyone had a right to a short bonanza, but holidays with pay were not available to all until 1938. Holidays had to be budgeted and saved for, and the comic cards inferred that at the end of them everyone was happily 'broke' but the bacchanalian experience had been worth it. 'If I had another sixpence I'd stay another week and let Father and Mother go home alone!' says one child to another. 'I don't want to leave,' says the little boy being yanked from the beach by an umbrella handle. 'I'm coming home by road,' says the skint holidaymaker sitting on the suitcase he's hitched to the back of a coach. Walter reveals on the back of this card, 'We are having a ripping time and are nearly spent up.' The young miss on the promenade revealing her stocking tops remembers the wash-day chores. 'Fifty weeks here and two weeks at work would suit me better.' 'Get as close to nature as you can this holiday!' says the Peeping Tom – a windy day is still a heaven sent opportunity to see even more of the girls' legs. 'The devil's in this wind – bless him!' *(Plate 75)*

There is an air of disbelief that the working class should be fortunate enough to enjoy the sheer hedonism of being by the briny. 'Tell me more! Tell me more!! Tell me more!!!' enthuses the young flapper to the old salt; 'W' writes on the back, 'George is inquiring why you have not sent him a postcard so have sent one for you to forward to him — do *not* put it in an envolope.' (sic). One speculates on the kind of card that 'W' selected. The Victorian objectors to the 'open' message would have disapproved anyway. The middle-aged as well as the young succumb to the delights of sea-bathing. Pa and ma with bucket and spade 'Carry on like a couple of kids at Cleethorpes.' Grasping little Willie firmly, they tiptoe across the unfamiliar sand to the sea, joyfully announcing, 'We'll soon be in the swim.' Ern writes, 'Just fancy me going in for this sort of thing an' no frills too. Am I having a gay time?' 'Be careful' says the caption above a pneumatic, middle-aged couple — 'There's no age limit here.' 'It's romance at a glance.' adds the sender. *(Plates 76, 73)*.

The old double entendre is still made to work. The voluptuous lady in striped bathing dress holds up some seaweed as the water laps round her crotch. 'I'm sure it's going to rain, my seaweed's quite wet,' she says coyly. *(Plate 74)*. One's 'seat' is the target for endless fun. So are parlour-maids,

114

lady's maids, chambermaids and waitresses. The war had opened up new jobs for women, who had made up one third of the work force. Domestic service was no longer the only opportunity for a working girl – but it died hard. The black and white maids' uniforms were a left-over from Mrs Beeton's day when the dresses of the maids and buttoned jacket of the boot and messenger boy were standardised in imitation of the livery which male servants had worn in the stately homes of yesteryear. The housemaid and parlourmaid 'should wear a scrupulously clean dress, thick white muslin aprons, neat caps . . . not rosettes of lace and ribbon which give a fast look to a servant and an air of vulgarity, to the house where such inappropriate costume is permitted.'

McGill dressed his maids in the appropriate uniform of the 1920s and 1930s – the fast look he gave them himself. They appear to have been considered fair game for postcard jokes, a sort of 20th-century left-over from the old droit du seigneur? The 1907 chambermaid looking through the key-hole and assuring the next lodger the occupant wouldn't be long, landed a hapless stationer with a £20 fine – but this card was updated by 1918 and again in 1950. 'Why don't you knock before you open the door?' says the half-dressed man. 'It's all right sir; I looked through the key-hole first!' replies the brazen chambermaid. The maid in cap and petticoat protests, 'Mum you told me to serve the tomatoes undressed but I'll not take off another stitch if I lose my job!' The diner by the sea grasps the waitress and declares, 'There's always something nice with your meals where I'm stopping – at Rhyl,' – but it could just as well be Ramsgate or Rottingdean. 'What are you doing Mary?' shouts the mistress from the top stair. 'Just pressing Master's trousers Mum' says Mary from the Master's lap. (*Plates 115-17*)

For both sexes the seaside seems to hold out the promise of a release of hidden libido. 'Don't you wish you'd left the wife at home?' say the bathing belles to the captivated onlooker being dragged away by his distinctly unattractive battle-axe of a missus.

People were experiencing the freedoms and frustrations of the motor-car, later aptly christened by a more permissive society the 'passion wagon'. 'I wonder where I shall go when I get where I'm going?' There are alarms and excursions, vehicles plunging into the sea, off the cliffs, down the hill or having to be pushed. The charabanc, which had replaced the horse drawn omnibus and the four-horse brake, whizzes past the sign post, 'To the cemetery,' out of control. 'We don't know where we're going but we're on our way.' Other passengers shove their charabanc up hill, 'It's taken some trouble to get here but it's worth it.' Holidaymakers cling to the platform of open-topped buses and trams on their way to the bandstand and promenade, or request a fat gent to give up his seat for three ladies. There is a spirit of adventure — riding in close proximity, crammed with others on crowded charabancs, trams and trains was all part of it. 'It'll take a lot to make me leave Blackpool,' says the huge lady being squeezed through the door of the cheap trip train. It was all part of the grand saturnalia which Donald McGill pictured; he took it all in his stride. He also made us laugh at the craze for crosswords, and at precocious kids. 'Wouldn't you like to go to heaven Myrtle?' 'No-o-o I've just come from there!' 'Remember Darling, though I take the candle away there will always be an angel with you.' 'Well Mum, I'd much rather you took the angel an' left the candle.'

The captions are often witty but some of the drawings made between 1916–30 are brilliant. As an artist this was McGill's own golden age.

5
The 1930s-1960s

McGill may have done his most artistic work in the 1920s but judged by the response of the postcard buying public, the 1930s – 60s was his golden age. The seaside cards began to dominate his output. Many resorts had become vast playlands – with piers and pierrots, rock and donkeys, boating lakes and tunnels of love. The seaside amusement complex mirrored the trippers' expectations and was called 'Playland', 'Funland', 'Wonderland' or 'Dreamland'. Billy Butlin opened his first holiday camp in Skegness in 1936 and holidays with pay were soon to be advertised as 'Holidays with Play'. A series of cards published for XL featured a knowing urchin but there were fewer hints of the grinding poverty that, for many, was a feature of the pre-war slump. One card of the 1940s shows a man with four children explaining to a friend, 'But we must keep having 'em, my wife's Maternity Benefit if the only income I've got!' *(Plate 101)* One mainly gets the impression of eternal sunshine, healthy pink flesh, carefree days, clean white cliffs and litter-free beaches. A sniff of ozone acted like an aphrodisiac – one undressed and bathed, courted and canoodled. One could be part of a candy-floss cloud-cuckoo-land where cheerful anonymity produced the bathing belle, the Beauty Queen, the 'Card'.

'I'm not one of the Bathing Belles/Or Beauty Queen of the day/But a bottle of stout and a donkey ride/And I'm Queen of the May', says the well-built lady donkey rider brandishing her bottle.

With the new moon and the pier in the background the beach Romeo murmurs, 'The moon lights up the summer sea,/The stars in heaven shine;/And what a girl learns at her mother's knee/She soon forgets on mine!'

There is a general air of bonhomie. 'It must be grand without a doubt, the sands, the sea and dining out,' says the man, with his tie still on, but sporty in his striped blazer and 'dining out' on fish and chips. The 1930s was a time when the countryside was being opened up and explored, when sunbathing and naturism, hiking, hostelling, picnicking and cycling became popular, revealing new worlds to the workers and new subjects for McGill's cards. Father in straw boater, striped blazer and plus fours prompts his small daughter to ask, 'Is Daddy going to a fancy dress, Mummy?' *(Plates 81/82)*.

By 1939 McGill's five year contract with one Blackpool customer was for a million cards a year.

Blackpool holidaymakers were posting 35,000 cards a day and judging from the trite messages on the back – 'We're having a jolly fine time – plenty of nice girls down here,' 'We're having a grand time – lovely weather' – few of them anticipated the end of summer 1939 would see the beginning of the Second World War.

McGill continues to design cards which helped to make light of the situation (as in *Plates 83, 84).* 'I wish to interrogate you Madam,' says the ARP warden flashing his torch in the blackout on a mature lady. 'Go along, you naughty boy! Why, I'm old enough to be your mother!!' The soldier on leave replies to an enquiring matron, 'Do they make you tidy in the army, Ma? Why I got ten days CB just because they found a little bit of fluff under my bed!' The bride sits in bed with her gas mask on protesting ' – Mother told me that if I was a sensible girl I should take precautions.' A buxom lady clasps a soldier to her bosom murmuring, 'You know I've always got a soft spot for a soldier!' An outraged girl, with nipples rampant, says to the policeman, 'He grabbed my ration book and tried to pinch my personal points,' – a reference also to the allocation of points for clothing and other coupons.

Ill-fitting uniforms were again good for a laugh – 'Here's your kit,' bawls the quartermaster to the National Service recruit, ' – an' if there's anything that fits bring it back and I'll change it.' Later, the arrival of American Romeos brought forth the caption, 'Would you like to hear what the girl said to the American soldier?' 'No I don't want to,' says the pert Miss. 'That's right!!' says the boyfriend making a grab for her.

In the end, however, the restrictions of paper meant that inferior board had to be used and, with the bombing in 1940 of the firm's premises in Ivy Lane, McGill found it impossible to continue He had moved to Guildford and, after struggling to exist on his capital for a year, he finally took a job as a temporary clerk with the Ministry of Labour until 1944, when he started drawing again. The 'New McGill Comics' carried the distinctive broken line border in red or blue and, in addition, a propaganda message on the back to encourage National Savings:

The War is won, your £.s.d.
Has helped to bring us victory
But saving still will pave the way
To that new world for which we pray.
KEEP SAVING FOR A RAINY DAY.

McGill's steadfast patriotism was blithely expressed in a postcard of two plump, pink-kneed bathing belles – one wears the Union Jack across her middle and the other the swastika across her

121

ample backside. On the back McGill had written:

> *Here's jolly good luck to Tommy and Jack*
> *Who fight for the red white and blue —*
> *And if one of them brings me a swastika back*
> *I shall know where to put that too.*

But one can always find McGill's own serious sentiments debunked. The huge lady soloist draped in the Union Jack announces that, 'Many a battle has been fought under this grand old flag,' whilst another card shows a little boy in his bath-tub with one hand submerged between his legs. He waves the flag with the other and says triumphantly, 'What we have we hold.' A companion card shows a naked tot shivering in the briny with his hand disappearing between his legs, 'I'm holding my own.' Another card on the same theme shows the waves lapping over a little boy sitting in the water, 'I've lost it,' he says, disconcerted. *(Plate 85)* This card was disapproved of in Hastings, whilst a much 'I've lost it,' he says, disconcerted. Amazingly, this card was disapproved of in Hastings, whilst a much later one showing two children by the water, bottoms exposed in the shape of, 'Two loving hearts by the sea' proved very popular and was counted as quite inoffensive.

Whilst infantile sexuality usually passed muster,

adult penis and bottom jokes were often transferred to nude statues to make them acceptable. The museum keeper strokes the bottom of a classical nude female and says to the lady visitor, 'Ma'am I've looked after 'em so long that I treat 'em same as if they were alive!' The cleaner, feather duster in hand looks at the hidden Hampton of the male statue and murmurs, 'What's the good of it? A dust catcher that's what it is.' Another Greek nude, labelled 'Man with discus', brings forth the relieved comment, 'There you are Gert – the Greeks had a word for it!' Snow falls outside the antique shop causing the china dog to say to the brass monkey, which is clutching the area of its unmentionables, 'I'm not surprised, it's cold enough!' One of the most popular cards in this genre shows a patient clothed only in a towel – a plaster lying on the floor behind him. 'What do you mean it dropped off?' asks a startled Doctor. McGill made the double entendre work for him, and for the customers it brought anything from simpers or giggles to thousands of belly laughs. *(Plates 88/90)*

Doctors, solicitors and professional men in McGill's world still wore grey pinstriped trousers, coloured waistcoats, black morning coats, bow ties, watch chains, shiny black patent pointed-toed shoes. The flighty young miss appears in a short, provocative, skin-tight, red sheath dress or tight red skirt and blouse with the bust and the bottom clearly defined. For variation the dress or skirt would sport white polka dots and be split at the back or sides revealing titillating thighs. He called it a combination between knee look and Dior's 1947 'New Look'. He told Eric Smithfield in *John Bull*, August 13 1949, that he had to sell '30,000 to 40,000 cards to show a profit' and spread the sales over ten years, so that it was important that current ladies' fashions did not date the cards. In an interview with Robert Jackson for *Illustrated* in 1954 he pointed out that his best sellers were simple cards. 'Take a woman with luscious curves, fore and aft. That's essential because people don't care for thin females — if they did, how would the manufacturers of falsies (bras) get a living? Dress your women in the brightest of colours. Add a caption capable of a double meaning and you have a comic card that by all the rules should sell at least 50,000 copies.' His major sales were in Blackpool, Scarborough and Brighton; he said that 'ultra-respectable towns, like Eastbourne and Frinton won't display them. They say they are vulgar — I suppose you might say that of Shakespeare? People who think joke cards are vulgar are mostly people who have forgotten how to laugh — they can only snigger.'

Vulgar or not, McGill continued to create a world

peopled by archetypes at once outrageous, yet recognisable. The nudist and the canny Scot still featured in the post-war gallery, the wind still lifting the kilt in the 1960s. The confident urchin of the 1930s in striped jersey and big brother's cap was gradually replaced by the better educated, better dressed, cleaner child of the post-war Welfare State. McGill revived some of his old kiddies' jokes, 'Why do you pull the pram instead of pushing it?' 'I can't stand the sight of this kid!!' The slum child's 'Don't keep sniffing like that, what do you think your sleeve's for?' seems a long way from such childish indignation as 'Birds and Bees, my foot! I put a bee in a cage with a bird and nothing happened!' There were fewer malapropisms, 'My old man suffered from conscription ever since 'e was demoralized from the Army!' says the wife revealing a bottle of castor oil. They reflected the times: 'What's the good of those Presbyterian Crossings − if you motorists are allowed to drive over them with impurity' (1942); 'My gal says she's got a diploma.' 'There, see what comes of going about with them foreigners.' The reply to the smart young miss sacked because she was redundant is, 'What a shame I'm sure no one would ever notice it.'

There were fewer references to bed-bugs and crowded boarding houses, but in the 1950s chamber pots were still in use as improvement grants had not yet turned every run-down cottage into the estate agents' 'cleverly modernised little house with all mod. cons.' From the pre-war card, 'I'm just going to look under the bed and see if there's a marauder there!' 'It's all right dear, it's round this side!' There was a post-war series of cards making fun of the all too real discomfort of finding oneself without any pot at all. McGill could always ingeniously ring the changes on the old joke. 'Shall I show you to the Bridal Chamber?' 'Nay, lad just show us the bedroom and we'll find that for ourselves!' An archway made up of bottles for the barmaid's wedding brings the wry comment, 'Fancy that! and the chambermaid's getting married next week!'

McGill still enjoyed parodying popular songs. For example, the visitor drawing a blank when he looks under the bed sings:

You miss the old homestead and faces you know
You miss scenes only memory can paint
But more than this that thing that you miss
When it ought to be there and it aint!

It is a simple world. Despite the movement at the end of the 1950s towards a more sexually liberated society many of those who were still embarrassed by their protuberances and their bodily functions found their anxieties lightened by laughter.

There are some references to radio and television but the technological advances of the post-war world do not feature prominently. The mother of quads asks her husband why he's never bought a television; the bikini-clad girl is deemed unsuitable as a candidate for 'What's my line?'; but McGill squeezes more humour out of organised games with sexy allusions to the use of balls, and such jokes as, 'Do you play tennis, Mrs Lovitt?' 'Oh, I play a shocking game!' 'Oh! do tell me what it is!'

McGill's pert young miss appears again and again − seductive and alluring with her retroussé nose, wavy hair, curvaceous figure, tilted hat and high-heeled shoes. 'Can I show you anything further, Sir?' she says invitingly as she mounts the shop steps to reveal her lovely legs. The sexual allusions are open and by today's standards seem innocent. 'I think they're wonderful' says the admirer in evening dress, examining a row of pearls but at the same time peeping down a pretty girl's cleavage. 'They're off!' she cries at the races as her knickers fall down. *(Plate 92, 94)*. Sharing a park bench with a pop-eyed companion she volunteers, 'Mother says I mustn't talk to strange men. But I can listen.' She leap-frogs in spotted bikini over her playmate, underneath the caption: 'Oh Mother dear, your little daughter is playing games she didn't oughter.'

Of course, McGill's snub-nosed, curvaceous

young miss was always irresistible. 'Drop me a line with all the news. I've got a little bit behind the Times down here' states the suitor, using the newspaper to camouflage his groping. The grand anonymity of the 'dirty weekend' gave rise to such cards as 'I'm "lying" on the beach. No Darling I'm not married' – from a prone Lothario. When asked if he believed in love at first sight, 'Do I? I've got to – I'm only down here for the weekend.' What price nostalgia when some large Brighton hotels are offering reduced rates to the Mr and Mrs Smiths because they believe the lifting of former restraints, has taken some of the daring and romance out of the illicit weekend? McGill caught the legendary risk in the atmosphere of the 'dirty' weekend by his card of the man waking up in a sweat, 'Good Heavens! I dreamt I was married!' he cries, as his girl clings nervously to the sheets. *(Plate 128)*

'I'm not flirting. I'm just keeping my hand in until you come down,' says the knowing young man with his arm round a cuddly girl. Reclining on the sands a siren says, 'I've sworn I'd never kiss a man till I was engaged.' 'Well that counts *me* out, doesn't it?' replies her man. 'Oh! I am engaged now!' Such were the typical sun-drenched flirtations of McGill's seaside world. The senders of cards reflect the sentiments: R.D. writes, 'Pleased to hear you are having such a good time, be careful on the boating lake, now you have clicked don't stay out late — and remember what I've told you about them there young men what rows!' 'Plenty of nice girls down here. No lidies.'

The smart young girl was also warned about learning to drive or taking a job. From the card sent in 1932 when Mother and Baby (Austin) were doing well, the myth of the disastrous woman driver was firmly implanted. The woman driver 'who signalled she was turning left — and turned left,' creates traffic havoc. 'You can go now dear — it's turned green,' says a woman passenger to a woman driver who has rammed a traffic light. 'I wish Madam, that you'd signal what you want to do!' calls an irate male driver. 'There's no signal for what I want to do!' says the woman driver, ecstatically leaping out of her car towards him. A common assumption in these pre-swinging '60s days was that what almost every woman wanted to do was trap a man into marriage.

McGill portrays marriage as a three-part joke. The first year he talks and she listens, the second year she talks and he listens, the third year they both talk and the neighbours listen. Humour about the honeymoon and the early years of married life seems comparatively gentle. For instance the doctor says to the wife of a sick man. 'I suppose you're giving him all he wants' 'Oh, Doctor,' she simpers, 'he's been too ill to think about anything of the sort.' Later, marriage brings out more bitter comment: 'The doctor said I was suffering from matrimonial thrombosis!' 'What on earth's that?' 'He said I'd married a clot!' The fraught wife says, 'I never thought you were so stupid when I married you.' 'Well you must have known I was a bit of a mug when I proposed!' is the rejoinder. The ageing wife, with sagging bosom, sighs over her wedding photo, 'I was only a slip of a girl when we were married!' 'Well, blimey, you've slipped a bit since!' The bandaged man in hospital when asked by the nurse if he was married, says – 'No – I was run over!' The cute young miss sums it all up with the verse:

Old or young, tall or short
Pick 'em out at random.
This bally town is full of men
Whose wives don't understand 'em!

Like the transformation scene in the pantomime, the wife gets larger and more domineering, the husband smaller and more acquiescent. 'Some people come down here for a holiday, and some bring their wives with them!' was not a new joke but it raised a steady laugh for more than 30 years. What wives they became! The Vicar calls and remarks to the husband, 'You surely admit the existence of a supreme and all powerful will?' 'Certainly I do, I married it!' The devil appearing to the bibulous spouse demands, 'Do you know who I am?' 'Of course I do. I married your sister!' is the reply. The desperate husband 'phoning the doctor to tell him the wife has dislocated her jaw suggests, 'If you're passing next week or the week after you might look in!' The wife becomes a nagging, unattractive termagant. The police sergeant looking at a missing wife's portrait, on being told the husband wants her found at once, asks, unbelievingly, 'Why?' *(Plates 99, 100, 105, 106)*

George Orwell thought the working class just accepted this transformation from honeymoon couple to battling middle age. Arthur Calder-Marshall believed the working class sacrificed their own interests for their children. Benny Green suggests marriage was a form of birth control by loathing which had its own bonds of dependency. Whether the bickering, middle-aged couples were highly exaggerated stereotypes or not, the cards were near enough to the truth to be bought in their thousands. The working class may have found it difficult to make ends meet but it could laugh at itself, and its situation. 'Come down here and leave your troubles (wife and baby) behind you.' The feeling of release from routine, 'Fifty weeks of work then two weeks of freedom' is something to savour:

> *Some girls work the whole week through*
> *And wash their smalls on Sunday,*
> *Thank goodness I'm not one of them –*
> *Well, not before next Monday!*

There was a companion card for men, of course. The break was still worth saving for – 'Two weeks on the sand every summer and then two months on the rocks!'

It was a safe, boozy world which had produced more than its share of giggles by the 1960s. 'I shan't half catch it from the Missis. I didn't get home yesterday till today, and I shan't get home today till tomorrow' leers the old soak, whilst another's missus says, 'If ever I got into the condition you're in, I'd shoot myself!' 'Well, if you were in the condition I'm in you'd miss yourself,' is the cheery reply.

Just how far the boundaries of sentiment and humour had receded can be seen in McGill's parody of that gem of Victorian moral rectitude 'Little Jim', the dying collier's child written by Edward Farmer. The original lines were:

> *I have no pain dear Mother, now*
> *But oh! I am so dry;*

132

Just moisten poor Jim's lips again
And, Mother don't you cry.

McGill's last two lines, uttered by a hospitalised drunk having a transfusion from a beer barrel, are – 'Connect me to a brewery/And leave me there to die!' The card may have seemed, at first, outrageous to a generation brought up on the tag end of Victorian parlour poetry but, judging by its popularity, its very outrageousness was enough to produce a frisson which resulted in postcard sales.

Constance Ltd was still selling postcard jokes about innocent or flirtatious chambermaids in the early 1950s. Mary, being asked to take Mr Jones' bags down, looks expectantly at the man, not his suitcases. She is warned by a veritable virago that next time she sews a button on the master's trousers she must wait till he takes them off; she is also instructed not to turn the master's bed-clothes down until *after* he has got up. One's heart goes out to the girl in her undies, still wearing the traditional black and white maid's cap and looking at the text over her bed, 'Be prepared, for the Master cometh,' 'Look at that now! What's a poor girl supposed to do?' This card was withdrawn in the early '50s and cards revealing the parlourmaid's predicament were gradually supplemented by jokes about the post-war woman secretary/shorthand-typist. 'She wasn't much of a typist, but Oh! Boy! was she experienced!' The interviewee replies to the boss 'You don't think I'll do? Don't think I'll do what?' Looked at from the 1980s the assumption that the lovely young secretary would be inefficient has a sexist ring. Equal opportunities legislation was a long way away. The smart young boss says to the new girl in the office 'You really must learn to use the typewriter. The people in the office are beginning to talk.' *(Plate 98)*

Whilst the secretary was often assumed to be inexperienced, the tradesmen were assumed to be worldly-wise voyeurs. The broad innuendo still had its place. The fireman and window cleaner were assumed to know all about kissing and vital statistics; the painter was ready to touch up the place, 'where my husband put his hand last night'. The old lady surprises the man on his ladder with an invitation to touch up her 'old fashioned whatnot'. The curate and the vicar still play an important role in life but remain naive, out of touch with the realities of marriage, copulation and what was in the pre-pill days, the almost inevitable pregnancy. The 1927 card, 'Oh! my dear Curate, we didn't know what sin was in our village, until you came,' was revamped in 1949, as was the splendid 1937 card on the sermon about foolish virgins, 'I'll never be one again,' says the young

134

1950s woman. *(Plates 103, 104)* The members of the Young Mother's League giggle as the vicar addresses them, 'I'm sorry to see so few "Young Mothers" here after all my efforts!'

Doctors appear to be no more worldly wise either, 'All you want is a little sun and air.' 'Oh, Doctor,' says the plump patient, looking coy, 'You naughty man! At my time of life!' *(Plate 109)*

Work is something to be avoided. Asked 'What's your husband's work?' the wife says, 'Well, Sir, he used to work at the gas works and make gas now he works at the water works and makes himself generally useful!'

The perky little wife becomes the horrendous mother-in-law who would need TIGER'S blood if she had to have a transfusion. The shopkeeper, asked if he has any postcards suitable to send to her, snaps curtly, 'No, and I shouldn't be allowed to sell 'em if I had.'

Fortunately for the public, shopkeepers were allowed to sell cards showing the whole gallery of McGill's characters. We can trace the anxious honeymoon couple becoming the obese pair, showing all their generous rotundity in striped bathing suits. 'What's this inflation they talk about?' say two fat drinkers with outsize bellies. Another two, blissfully resting their pot bellies by a café table, cause the waitress to giggle, 'Now which of you is going to be Mother?' The fat lady with the huge rear end confides in her dentist, 'The top set's artificial but the bottom's my own.' Pneumatic busts give rise to a whole series of innuendoes. 'Brassiere? Yes, Madam; what bust?' asks the shop assistant helpfully. 'Ee luv, nothing bust, it just wore out!' The humour of McGill did not wear out – he used and re-used the old music hall jokes, the wit of the BBC Light Programme, the stories of the pub raconteur, and he created a rebellious and Rabelaisian world. His gigantic bosoms, bottoms and bellies bloom all over his cards, comforting the slightly fat purchaser with the thought that she's not that fat, the hen-pecked husband that he's not that hen-pecked, the honeymoon couple that they are not that stupid, the toper that he never gets quite that drunk, the parents of the awful child that their little darling is not that bad.

According to psychologists much of our humour is a way of releasing tensions which exist as a by-product of society's repressions. Our very existence is a result of our parents' sexual activity, however much various moral pressure groups might seek to make the subject taboo. Laughter is caused by situations which expose or exploit the taboos, the conventions and the pretensions of our society. Without the framework of accepted and sometimes ridiculous rules to be broken the jokes would not be funny. At times Donald McGill's jokes were ribald and vulgar but they were also witty and sometimes very funny indeed — his most valuable contribution to a world which has always shown itself to be in need of laughter.

6
The Postcard Publishing Business

McGill could have spent every hour of his long life drawing and painting, but without the drive and energy of men of entrepreneurial spirit his labours would have been of no avail. There is no doubt that he became less rich than those who took the creations of his pen and brush, converted them into postcards, and persuaded shopkeepers that the public would buy them in one of the earliest forms of self-servce.

The path between drawing board and public has never been an easy one, with complications and snags for even the successful, which conform to the axiom that 'if it were easy, they would all do it'.

If started today, the marketing of cards would have been backed by the findings of social and market surveys; 'the product' would have been tailored to meet the requirements of the population groups most likely to buy, and outlets, point of sale material and sales promotion would have all been planned, with accountants in the background costing and monitoring the enterprise. Not so in 1905 as more often than not marketing, production and organisation was the work of one man, or perhaps a partnership.

The EC1 area of London was the site of many of the publishing enterprises. The proprietors were frequently of German-Jewish origin for the postcard owes much to German expertise in production and printing. In fact, much of the printing continued to be done in Germany, though the products were essentially for sale in Great Britain.

Generally speaking, the artists were freelance operators who sold their designs outright to a publisher whose object was then to maximise the return on his investment. The name of the game in printing is firstly that the initial run shall justify the cost of plate-making and that the repeat shall justify setting up again and further amortise initial expenses. In practice, the public proved remarkably fickle, and the 'best-seller' in one area has been the sadness in another shopkeeper's wallet. Designs dated with events and old favourites might well mysteriously stay in place in the display racks.

With the possible exception of the time when cards were bought from new as 'collectables' (as older cards are now) the element of selectivity and actual searching for a particular design in comic cards was lacking. The sale depended on the mixture of availability and impulse. Once the artist had done his job with brush and paint and further had provided a joke acceptable to the prospective buyer, the most important thing of all was that the publisher could persuade the shopkeeper to display his card in preference to the competition.

I am concerned with the relationship between publisher and creator, specifically with the men on whom Donald McGill depended, and his own involvement in marketing at an age when most men would have opted for the rocking chair.

McGill's own statements and letters raise the curtain on these relationships only by a very little. He was not a man who would criticise or blackguard anyone and, for that reason, his few words of comment are worthy of note, together with the testimony of perhaps more forthcoming and outspoken witnesses. The central characters involved in putting McGill's work before the public were Robert McCrum and Joseph Ascher, of the firms of Inter Art Co. and D. Constance Ltd respectively. Max Honnest and the Hutson Bros. were also significant though short lived relationships. As the intermittent but seemingly ever present Svengali, Joseph Ascher must rank as the most important and his relationship with the artist over 40 years could surely warrant a psychologist's attention. Was Joseph Ascher Donald McGill's alter ego?

It may assist collectors if I quote McGill's own dating for his various publishers. I cannot promise that this makes easier the identification of cards which may have been issued after he severed the connection, which is well illustrated by the fact that the premier collector of McGill in UK has 8,483 cards, as at August 1983, and has identified no less than nine varieties of imprint for the years 1935 to 1965.

1904-1907 Part-time freelance
1907-1908 Full-time freelance
1908-1910 Hutson Bros as 'A Partner' (H.B.)
1910-1914 Joseph Ascher as a freelance but 'contracted to do so many sketches per week'
1914-1931 Inter Art Co.
1931-1936 Full-time freelance
1936-1952 D. Constance Ltd (J Ascher) As previously, 'a gentleman's agreement'
1952-1962 Under (written) contract to D. Constance Ltd for sketches, with salary for administrative duties.

Up to 1968 McGill designs were reprinted with the 'Constance' imprint, firstly from Beach Road and then High Street, Littlehampton. After 1972, some old cards were overprinted giving a London, SW6 address and a limited number of 'I've lost it' (with apostrophe misplaced) were in circulation as a greeting card.

The variation of marks of identity on cards of earlier years is very wide indeed. Such legends as 'New McGill' with full address are obvious and refer to cards produced from 1936 onwards.

The following have been seen on one or many genuine McGill cards; but pirating and plagiarisations were not unknown:

Ascher (sometimes Asher) J. A. Co. – Kismet – D. Constance Ltd, Selwell

Bamforth USA – Bamforth Prohibition Comics (Joint Bamforth/Inter Art Enterprise)

Burn Bros – B.B.

Eyre and Spottiswoode – Woodbury – E & S

Hutson Bros – H.B. (commonly referred to as Hudson Bros)

Inter-Art Co. – Comique and many other series

Newman Bros., Glasgow

Mortimer Bros., London

Morris & Co., Liverpool

Pictorial Postcard Co. – Empire – E.S.

J. Thridgould and Co. – J. T. & Co.

Woolstone Bros – W. B. – Milton – Elite

XL Series – though fairly numerous no link known to named company.

The life of a collector is not a simple one and, in addition, the following are to be found – British

Product, British Made Throughout, ERS, Made in England, Printed in Holland, Printed in Saxony, W, PS.

In the atmosphere of the early part of the century it is not surprising that Max Honnest-Reddlich dropped the hyphenated part of his name by the time he set up his Pictorial Postcard Co. in 1903. I discovered that the family name seems exclusive in England today, with or without two n's, and there is a marvellous esoteric joke somewhere in the fact that the Nationwide British Telecom Directories indicate that the only 'honest' man in the UK lives in Scotland — do you like it Donald?

Honnest's business was not exclusively in comic varieties. In common with all card publishers wide exploitation was the norm. Certainly amongst the smaller people it was an accepted practice that the local representative sallied forth with his camera to secure the views for the following seaside season. My friends in view-card collecting tell me that the use of the box-Brownie to secure some original pictures, is all too apparent.

It is now reasonably certain that Honnest was McGill's first publisher and 1904 the date. The company was relatively short lived and the transfer of McGill's work to Hutson Bros is coincidental with the winding up and the fact that some of the Pictorial Postcard Co's assets were taken over, including

McGill. Max Honnest enjoys the distinction, together with Joseph Ascher, of being interned on the Isle of Man in the 1914-18 War. In the case of Joseph it is to be hoped that his residence qualifications later weighed in the favourable censoring of his published cards.

McGill's 'partnership' with the Hutson Bros, which lasted two years, was only in the nature of an exclusive right to the designs, as was the continuation of contact with Percy Hutson, a representative for Honnest. McGill is reported to have said that he found the relationship between the brothers uncomfortable. 'Womanising and drinking' were the words used but it must be remembered that notwithstanding his saucy output, McGill himself described his own standards as Victorian. It is almost commonplace for dual directors and brothers to argue and disagree, and it is not at all unlikely that the blandishments of Joseph Ascher, who was a customer of the Hutsons, hastened McGill's departure. The two years with Ascher might well have gone on continuously until Ascher's death were it not that he was interned as an enemy alien in 1914.

" What's this 'inflation' they talk about? "

I have no pain, Dear Mother, now
But, oh, I am so dry
Connect me with a Brewery
And leave me here to die!

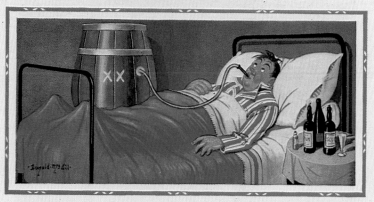

My new bathing dress   What you can't see of me
Is quite a success—   Of course you must guess.

   "Je crois que je fais sensation!"

" My new bathing dress,
Is quite a success ;
What you can't see of me
Of course you have to guess ! "

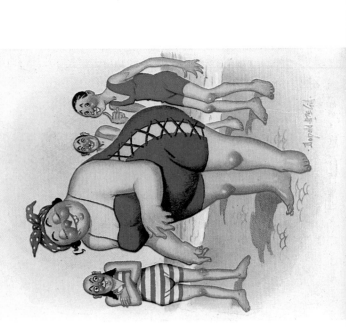

"CAN'T SEE MY LITTLE WILLY?"

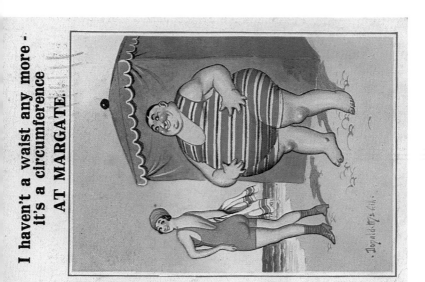

I haven't a waist any more -
it's a circumference
AT MARGATE.

Fifty weeks here and two weeks at work would suit me better.

Some poor devils toil all day
A livelihood to seek,
Thank goodness I'm not one of these —
At least, not this week!!

Pa and Ma carry on like a
couple of kids
AT CLEETHORPES.

I'm sure it's going to rain - my
seaweed's quite wet.

The devil's in this wind — bless him !
Le diable est dans ce vent - qu'il soit loué !

TELL ME MORE!
TELL ME MORE!!
TELL ME MORE!!!

"EVERYBODY'S DOING IT"

WHY SHOULDN'T WE

Donald McGill.

IF I HAD ANOTHER SIXPENCE
I'D STAY ANOTHER WEEK

AND LET FATHER AND MOTHER
GO HOME ALONE !

Donald McGill.

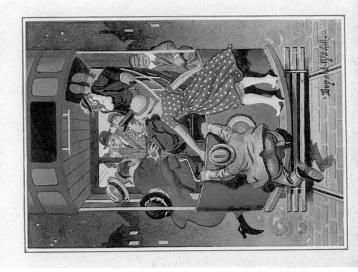

We enjoy riding on the
promenade

"CROSSWORDS"
"I daren't go upstairs till
I've solved this one!"

"Is daddy going to a fancy dress, mummy?"

"No dear, but we're at the sea-side now, you know!"

It must be grand without a doubt, the sands, the sea and dining out.

" Here's yer kit, an' if there's anything that fits, bring it back an' I'll change it ! "

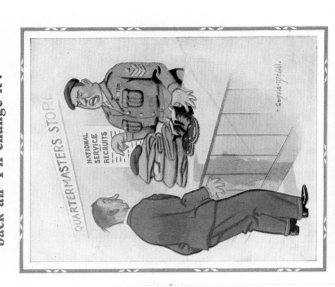

" Many a battle has been fought under this grand old flag ! "

"What we have we hold!"

I'VE LOST IT

THEY KICKED HIM FROM THE NUDIST CLUB,
THEY DIDN'T SAY "GOOD-BYE,"
BECAUSE HE TURNED UP ON PARADE,
WEARING HIS OLD SCHOOL TIE!"

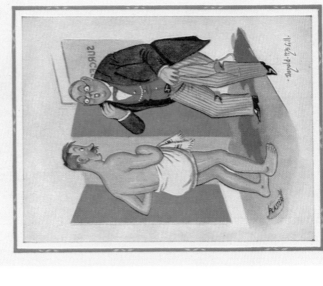

"What d'you mean - it
dropped off?"

"I'm just going to look under the bed
and see if there's a marauder there!"
"It's all right, Dear—it's round this
side!"

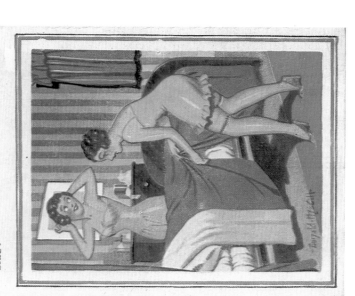

"There you are, Gert – the Greeks
had a word for it!"

"I think they're wonderful!"

"Drop me a line with all the news, I've got a little bit behind the Times down here!"

"Can I show you anything further, Sir?"

"They're Off!"

"It must be awful for a woman
to be tempted !"
"It's far worse not to be !"

"Do you believe in love at first sight ?"
"Do I ! I've got to — I'm only down here
for the week-end !!"

Inter-Art Company

A collector quotes the number of McGill cards published by the Inter-Art (International Art Co) as 3,670, out of a known total output of 8,996, many in the well-named 'Comique' series. Robert McCrum and his wife ran this very successful publishing enterprise from London addresses and the warehouse near their own home in Nassau Road, Barnes, London SW13.

I have only found two descriptions of McCrum – 'a bit of a drinker, but kind to children' and 'Romeo McCroom'. This would surely be an obituary acceptable to many men. My husband's memory is as reliable or otherwise as anybody's and his childhood memories of Florence House, as he went on his way to school, include the sound of printing presses, as this was the site for production rather than just distribution and storage. McGill's association with McCrum was a long one and he paid regular weekly visits to Barnes as well as attending the roof-top parties on University Boat Race Day. The continuing interplay between publisher and artist is well illustrated by the changes of style and the response to market forces. By the end, the fat ladies were becoming dominant. This is indeed quoted as the reason for McGill's departure. '. . . there was a clean-up and they would not let me draw people with red noses, women in bathing costumes with cleavage, it was so ridiculous I resigned.'

Joseph Ascher and D. Constance Ltd

Joseph Ascher returned from Germany in 1934 and by 1936 the links forged originally became akin to bonds – for McGill anyway. He had a 'gentleman's agreement' and a nominal (and useless) single shareholding in D. Constance. Together with Ernest Maidment as manager, it could be said that Ascher used them to 'front' his organisation with respectability; this is far too simplistic a view. Joseph Ascher was the man who marketed McGill as he is universally known, the essentially 'seaside' comic cards, the distinctive 'New McGill Series'. His flare was to use an artist by name, to pick on one as talented, loyal and honest as McGill and to make a very great deal of money in so doing.

When Josef Ascher originally came over from Germany in 1902 (04?) he anglicised his christian name, and the 'c' was dropped out of his surname (by him) intermittently. Joe Ascher was the archetypal travelling salesman; I have seen the list extended but it is certain that he represented his father's mask factory in Lliminau (sic) Thuringia, and sold jokes, sneezing powder and carnival novelties. His German identity card for his return to England in 1934 included the description 'Fine Art Publisher' and the original German connection with postcards is obvious.

From 1936 the figures for the Constance Co. do not show prosperity and McGill seems to have been convinced that things were difficult. He later quoted the figure of a £365 loss for the first year of trading, with an authority bred of the need to maintain the fiction of a participation which Ascher simply did not promote with him. Looking at the records for the post-war years and adding knowledge of the publisher's happy knack of massaging figures it is reasonable to doubt that things were perhaps not so bad for Ascher just before the War.

The War Damage claim for 3/4 Ivy Lane, EC4, is enlightening if only because it sets a definite figure on the valuation Ascher put on McGill's original work. It would be reasonable to assume that the value at the time would be not less than that paid for each work and would certainly take account of what the District Valuer would stand.

From the city and its surroundings there must have been hundreds if not actually thousands of claims. The Valuers acting for the Government were in this case Kenneth Elms & Co of Fenchurch Street, responsibility finally passing to a Mr O'Kelly at the

Strand office of the District Valuer. O'Kelly solemnly interviewed Ascher, having first requested information to enable him to examine salvage from the bombing. The event occured on 29 December 1940 (the very raids are in my diary); but the request to see the charred remains came more than 18 months afterwards, on the 7 July 1942. None can accuse our Civil Service of a lack of tenacity.

101 of McGill's originals were lost to Hitler's bombs, the value put on them by Ascher was £126.12s – in 1983 terms about £18 per piece. There were only 6,000 cards claimed to be in stock with a present-day value of not much over £70. The quantity is a lot less than the small retailer would expect to take in for the season today but there is a reasonable explanation for this low stock. Whatever his failings, Ascher was a very good business man, he would get orders 'on the book' if at all possible at the end of one season; but the buying of the board and the print orders for the next season could be delayed until the last moment. He often sold to the trade from originals which were not then in course of printing.

By the time of the bombings of Ivy Lane, restrictions were coming in fast and there was difficulty with the supply of board; but it is shown clearly that the December stock was valued at about one-fifth of the cartons which were to contain them and about three times as much as Else Ascher's

Zigarettes (sic). The boss and his wife lived on the job and a claim for Else's two bras (12s/6d = £9 each) was lumped in with McGill's drawings. I hear Donald's laugh from afar, happy to hear that one creative work is nearly equal to the value of three bras.

The supply of board became impossible. As mentioned previously, at 65 years of age Donald took a job with the Ministry of Labour, 'after living for a year on capital'. Ascher was registered as an alien and had his movements checked and restricted; but he nevertheless took up British citizenship in 1948. He seems to have kept his head above water during the war and in the immediate post-war period with sales of the few greetings cards and such like which he could wholesale. The few short years from 1944 to his death were spent in a spurt of entrepreneurial fervour.

Ascher energetically promoted McGill's cards; 80% of the sales were made by him. He oversold, pushed, cajoled and gave extended credit. He used whatever board he could find, combined the sale of perfume (without much smell) and lipstick (which did not) and any other goods which he could lay hands on. He was soon 'into property' and when he died there was such an awful mess left behind that even the lawyers and accountants had cause to wonder at the wisdom of earning their fees in the Herculean labour of sorting it all out.

He married twice, both times to non-Jewish ladies and he was viewed as everything from a 'lovely funny man' to 'an awful fellow' and 'an untidy, hairy gorilla'. He adored and mourned his well-built and gentle Catholic wife Else. He cared much about his own parents and in-laws. He was a terrifying, awful driver and his car accidents and bumps were legion. He sent flowers and a tender note to one who got in the way of his car. He was crude, uncouth and very greatly concerned for the welfare of an adopted infant, who was only four when Else died.

At his death Ascher had willed virtually all to his adopted boy. There was nearly £7,000 (£45,000 in 1983 terms) contained in a safe deposit box, there was a further £3,000 of liquid assets, three houses which were mortgaged, but the loan was covered by Marks and Spencer shares. D. Constance had an outstanding tax liability of £10,000 and as an accountant was provoked to remark 'some individual proprietors do tend to confuse their personal affairs with that of the limited company they control'. In Joseph Ascher's case this was the understatement of the century.

One other professional gentleman, reviewing the affairs of the limited company, assessed its goodwill value as nil. Obviously he had to take a cautious view of McGill's ability to continue drawing 'winners', though his almost stuttering incredulity at Joe's methods of business and his notes of the legacy in dead stock, make it crystal clear just what a task awaited the overseeing Estate Trustees and the new 'partnership' of Maidment with McGill. The latter ready and willing to work on and to allow himself to become more involved than ever before, at 77 years of age!

I have asked time and time again how the gentle McGill could have possibly tolerated this situation with the buccaneering Ascher. Of course, Ascher's life activities were not entirely tied to McGill's designs but there is not the slightest doubt that the profits from comic cards were very good and that the figures for McGill's earnings make it clear that he was underpaid for the wealth he helped to produce. Ascher left McGill no token of regard. Ironically, Donald did not qualify as 'an employee' in the terms of the will and therefore did not receive even the four weeks salary left to the small staff by their employer. On Ascher's death the Trustees were concerned only to do the duties laid upon them in the upbringing and maintenance of the adopted son. What has been described above with regard to the chaos left behind is an understatement not an exaggeration. The declared figures show that the business was in decline. One-man controlled businesses are marvellous whilst the one man is right on top of the job. Let his attention divert or his methods be too generally extreme and the result can be a quite speedy deterioration.

Mr Ernest Maidment, together with McGill, formed the management team and coped manfully with the problems left by the late proprietor, the movement for censorship, the obscenity cases and 100% Purchase Tax (now VAT). The Trustees overseeing the operation were very understanding and one of their first acts was to give McGill a more respectable remuneration. Regrettably, within a few years, there was talk that perhaps he was not really earning his keep. I am very glad indeed that McGill, who actually volunteered to take less for his sketches, was not alive when the company benefited to the tune of (equivalent 1983) £12,000 from the sale of his sketches at Sotheby's. His family was not offered one – such is the way of business.

On McGill's death and the introduction of new management and shareholding, the comic range with the 'Pedro' imprint was introduced. The now 'dated' McGills were phased out and fewer and fewer were printed and, by 1968, all production had stopped.

In 1973 what stocks of cards remained, together with blocks, an archive and the copyright, which had been specifically reserved when the sale at Sotheby's was made, were sold as one package to my husband, Basil Buckland, and Michael Tickner. They bought out of affection and interest in Donald McGill, with a possible business interest but only indefinitely hoping to recoup cost. A booklet was published based on research completed at the time. My husband's colleague has since retired from the enterprise.

D. Constance Ltd is still thriving. The proportion of comics now marketed compared to view cards almost exactly reverses the proportion sold when McGill was the one artist and his work gave the company the major part of its turnover. Today the need for constant change and fresh approaches to keep sales buoyant is reflected in changes of artists to meet the changing demands.

The final connection with the founder was severed in 1979 when the Ascher Estate trustees sold out their interest to the installed Management/shareholders.

The accounts for 1949 quote Joseph Ascher's salary as £2,000, his 'drawing' from the Company as £3,452. If the very reasonable view is taken that the average drawings over three years would be fairer, then the figure is £2,632. Further, (tongue in cheek) we must assume that all car and other expenses were duly spent and not used by Ascher personally. We arrive at a return to Ascher for his efforts of (1983 equivalent) £18,000 which I think to be a very satisfactory sum for a business run privately from a house in Streatham – though perhaps I am just wary of company accounts.

At no time, even with the proper contract from the Ascher Trustees, did Donald McGill receive much in excess of £5,000 a year (1983 equivalent) and Flat 7 at 36 Christchurch Road, Streatham rent free, his tax (such as it would be at that time) plus a paid telephone. I regard it as virtually unthinkable that he ever received any non-declared cash during the whole of his career – he was just not 'that sort of chap'.

McGill's patent honesty shines through in a dishonest world. He wrote '. . . it would be very damaging to my credit and prestige if it now appeared that I had been for many years a sort of underpaid hack or sweated labour. It would also be unpleasant if this got about among my friends and acquaintances – and the tradespeople . . .' This was 1954 and this dear man was living in Streatham, a widower aged 79. He was patently McGill, gentleman – no match for the man he outlived by eleven years but who, I fear, must be judged to have lived off him.

Card Sales, Postings and Earnings

It is said that the day of written communication is dead but this is hardly born out by the evidence. The Post Office is now unable to supply figures due to mechanisation and the advent of the two-tier post system which eliminated the differential rate applicable to cards in 1968. My local postmaster believes that the despatch of cards per se has dropped considerably over the years. Indeed, the figures for 1960 of 35,000 cards per day in the small seaside place where I live are probably not matched today. I well remember postal boxes being full to overflowing at Christmas time in my then London suburban residential area. At the seaside such sights were commonplace in the summer season, though boxes were emptied with greater frequency.

Although such boom times for cards are gone forever, sales are very buoyant indeed. Whether view cards or comics the single unit four sided stands seen outside many seaside shops turn over 10-15,000 cards in the short British season and there is every reason for thinking that these results are multiplied many times on the busiest sites.

Selling cards is a business and the majority of shopkeepers are quite unsentimental about the stock they buy, judging their spending on the past and on possible sales at the best profit. For some, the rack of cards at the front of the shop is the means by which the public are brought in to pay for a self-selected purchase and to be tempted into further and more substantial buys. It is an observable fact that the sale of comics takes place in the greatest quantity near to the beach and the places of entertainment, with view cards in the main shopping area. This is not an unalterable rule but is fairly consistently observed.

Card publishers are naturally coy about quoting any figures but I have made a most careful assessment relating to the New McGill series in 1954, by applying conservative estimates to extrapolate from cash received in comic sales to numbers sold, I calculate that in 1954, 4,000,000 cards left D. Constance Ltd and this in a year which, from the point of view of the shareholders, was poor. Others have quoted McGill sales in his lifetime and it is not my object to join the chorus; but if my figures are on the conservative side, as I believe them to be, and knowing that 1954 was the beginning of the end, one must marvel at the distribution given to one product sold primarily in the six to eight weeks of summer.

To illustrate the difficulties for traders, I must quote the words of the daughter of a stall holder, who for some years traded near Madame Tussauds in London. He included in his stock for some time a range of McGill cards but, in conversation, I gathered that he had abandoned them for the sale of views. I was naturally curious and queried his reasons. It had nothing to do with obscenity or public complaints, nor with the fact that sales were good and profitable. It had very much to do with the large crowd of 'lookers' attracted to the jokes, who did buy one or two, but they caused just too much obstruction to the easier buyer (often foreign visitors) of views by the pack and higher value gift lines. This is the sort of problem the modern marketeer loses sleep to solve when he has a perfectly saleable but low value product. In the end the shopkeeper is very much the judge of what we will buy.

Some McGill enthusiasts may note the omission of certain often quoted figures for both McGill's earnings and card sales. In the case of those which are quoted, every effort has been made to verify them; but when millions are involved this is really not easy. I have chosen to omit, where there is any doubt, and hope that the confirmed figures, particularly with regard to earnings, give an accurate overall picture.

7
The Censor

This book does not attempt to be a social history; but McGill's world was part of the real world and in many ways the comic card reflected and recorded attitudes and changes as they occurred.

I shall, perhaps, be on highly contentious ground; but so was McGill. Opinions may vary as to McGill's artistic merit; but contention here is as nothing beside the disputes which he generated in his day by expressing opinions where matters of sex were involved.

If I show up as an all too tolerant liberal – so was the artist. He could, in his work, oscillate between being a champion of the working class and a pillar of class-fixed establishment. In one field, however, it is to his credit that up to the ripe old age of 87 he thought of human activity in the framework of sexual activity. Please, fellow Women's Libbers, I know that he could express chauvinist ideas and that, as years went by, he was behind the times; but I am sure he actually liked women.

It is a certainty that if you express publicly opinions on matters sexual, and continue to do so for many years, there will come a time (in the UK anyway) when the hand of the Establishment and Establishment Law will be upon you. It is a pity that McGill had to face the storm in his 70s. He was genuinely upset by the blows when they came and, though his court appearances found him apparently calm and unruffled, he had anxieties, not the least of which was that his true position as an exploited employee should be revealed during the proceedings.

Censorship as far as it affected McGill was the attempt to suppress the display and sale of comic cards thought, by those officials involved, to be detrimental to society. (This definition is really only in part applicable to the voluntary censoring committees.) As far as the UK is concerned, the first effective censor was the Post Office, but once accepting an item as suitable for transmission it has stuck to its task of safely delivering the King's/Queen's Mails, notwithstanding the powers given by the 1908 Act which continue modified through the changes of status of the Post Office.

I remember a letter in my local paper, many years ago, calling on the postman to be saved from the evil of delivering what were delicately referred to as preventatives. No action seems to have followed, nor any with regard to comic postcards.

The reluctance of the GPO to act as censor is matched by the absence of any major movement to suppress the card, as evidenced by a lack of

Parliamentary interest in this respect. Seaside towns were the seat of unrest; the fumes and fury generated now seem to have been very much 'parish-pump'. The popular papers showed only passing interest and by and large took a stance of amused observation and toleration rather than condemnation. The explanation for this lies in the seasonal nature of comic card sales. Just as it is hardly possible to become exercised about the 'scandal' of nude bathing in December, a campaign to suppress the comic card via Parliamentary action seems pretty lame by the time the House re-assembles in autumn.

Nevertheless, the comic card has been suppressed and censored with results as significant as any of the moves made against books, films and plays. Results were not only significant but very similar. The legendary 'dirty postcards' on offer to tourists in Europe and the Middle East and any derivatives sold in the UK cannot be seen as other than insignificant. Substantial enquiries have failed to establish direct reporting on extensive suppression of earlier comic cards produced by McGill and his contemporaries. Allowing for my own fallibility in this matter, I must further say that, notwithstanding second-hand reporting at a later date, I have no direct evidence of more than the most casual cases of seizure by individual Police forces in the 1930s.

In 1954 McGill wrote, 'During the whole course of

my career the Authorities have made no complaints about the postcards drawn by me with the following exceptions:

'1. In or about 1906 I recollect that an order was made for the destruction of one out of a very large number (in the North of England).

'2. In or about 1920 proceedings were taken against the retailers of two cards; but no order was made in respect of these cards.

'I do not recall any other proceedings until about 1950 when there were a few prosecutions; but the cards I had drawn were in the minority and a number of other publishers were concerned.'

Isle of Man

The unique nature of the Isle of Man sometimes referred to as Britain's Off-Shore Island of the North, is never better revealed than in its attitude to comic postcards. Its constitution and geography allowed it, unlike mainland Britain, to set up effective and community approved machinery to deal with what it saw as a social problem.

The first moves towards censorship were in the form of a voluntary code promoted by a former retailer of cards, with the active encouragement of the Church. Mr Hough's voluntary body of 1912 was succeeded by a statutorily constituted Censoring Committee by an Act of Tynwald in 1933. For 50 years this nominated body has been the arbiter of comic cards to be sold on the island. It is somewhat strange that the three man committee has worked without actual guidance from the Act as to what they should regard as obscene/objectionable or undesirable. Guidance may be sought from the Attorney General, and I have it on the authority of the Chairman that reference has been made to the dictionary for the meaning of that word 'obscenity'. In fact their duties were to examine all comic cards and to merely 'approve' or 'disapprove' of what they saw.

The chairman for 1953 was reported as having expressed the opinion that 'vicars were not suitable subjects for comic cards'. The Act provided that no card could be displayed without prior approval of the Committee and for (modest) penalties for so doing. The publishers of cards, before making any attempt to sell to retailers, submit three samples of each design to the Committee which meets on an ad hoc basis as the demand arises. The decision as to suitability or otherwise must be unanimous; two of the three members constitute a quorum.

The temptation to mock and to write this activity off as some wild aberration is all too easy and is simply not good enough. McGill and his publishers had problems in their day and I have on record the serious discussion that the Island should be ignored as a market due to, what the management saw, as the capricious and unreasonable rejection of one design against the approval of another.

The uniqueness of the IOM lies in the fact of the statutory backing for censorship. The first of the three sample cards is forwarded to the Chief Constable and forms the basis of any prosecution. Even recent residents running shops would very soon become aware of the mores of the society in which they traded. The Committee is effective in what it has set out to do and confident enough to actually celebrate its 50 years 'in business'.

In 1983 the Committee decided to examine its archive and to put on display a selection of cards which had been filed away as disapproved. This was a very bold and imaginative operation. David G. Swinton was commissioned to prepare a Golden Jubilee postcard, a pastiche of rejects of yesteryear. This was printed in its straight form and as a 'limited edition', signed by the president of the Manx Legislative Council and the whole Committee, then sold to the public. A tent was taken at the Tynwald Fair and the voluntary censors, together with the Secretary who is a civil servant, sold the cards whilst the Manx public and summer visitors were invited to laugh at what they had not been allowed to see (in the

IOM anyway) over five decades. They could also meet the censors who were observably well known and popular.

Throughout its life, individual members have served the Committee for anything up to 18 years and the present Chairman gives an original reason for the continuation of what might be taken to be an anachronism in the atmosphere of 1983. He expressed the thoughts that, 'The justification for the Committee resides in the respect we hold for ourselves and others. Examples of comic postcards continue to be submitted where humour is associated with, diminished or replaced by rudeness, vulgarity or obscenity. Whilst some may tolerate or enjoy such standards in private, so others are entitled to insist that public decorum is maintained. It is part of the Committee's responsibility to ensure that postcards on public display and sale are not in advance of current social standards and attitudes.' The Chairman is a school teacher, predominantly engaged in pastoral care and in common with the other censors, was relaxed and laughing. Since the Chairman has served the Committee for a total of 10 years it must be assumed that he does not experience difficulty in applying what he would see as principles for today, which may well seem near ridiculous 10 years hence.

Looking around the major resort town of Douglas I

gained the distinct impression that the Committee must now indeed be punch drunk by the overt crudity and poor humour of the cards they feel they must now 'approve'. The standard of some of these cards which are lacking any glimmer of subtlety would not have been acceptable to McGill even on an off-day.

In virtually every press interview McGill mentions the IOM Censoring Board. The £1 note toilet roll card was more a worry to the authorities for its accurate representation of currency than obscenity. The legal establishment can, however, show great delicacy and were reluctant to refer over boldly to the object to which the King's currency was being put.

It was in the 1950s that the publishers and shopkeepers were troubled by those who opposed cards dealing in human behaviour in a 'saucy', 'vulgar', or as they saw it, 'obscene' manner. Contrary to the popularly quoted influence of the 'Watch Committees', most Police action was based on the information laid by individuals and not any united move by Committees whose duties were so multifarious as to keep them well and truly occupied. Following diligent searches of Council Committee Minutes and finding only passing comment recorded, I have spoken to civic dignitaries with excellent recall of events who by no means substantiate stories of scandal and outrage involving direct action by Watch

Committees.

The situation of 30 years ago was that recovery from the 1939-45 War was still in its early stages, rationing was in force and was, in some particulars, harsher than conditions of actual wartime; but there were stirrings and efforts to achieve the 'freedom' for which we had fought. It is not too fanciful to contend that those who viewed with displeasure a world markedly different from that which they had known in the 1930s, were all too ready to condemn the plays of Osborne and Miller, the books of Braine and the irreverence of Dylan Thomas. It was a time of instability and perhaps it is not very surprising that in the atmosphere of the day the comic postcard formed for some, a facile focus for more complex worries.

It is an unhappy coincidence that it was on the death of Joseph Ascher that the rumblings of trouble increased. The Police are obliged to investigate when information is laid before them on questions of public order or morality. Since the judgement of what is or is not obscene is entirely subjective it is almost certain that if there was then the slightest cause for doubt the Chief Constable, totally dependent upon the goodwill of the powerful and influential in the community, would have little choice but to start up a legal process. This might end fairly quietly with a fine of a few pounds levied on a local shopkeeper in a Magistrates' Court or might result in a full scale trial at the

County Sessions bringing in the card publishers as well as the retailer, with matching extra publicity.

A flurry of these cases started to worry retailers and for their own protection they turned, naturally enough, to their Chambers of Trade or Commerce for advice. These were the media through which several 'Censorship Committees' were set up. It is a popular misconception that they had some sort of official standing and power, this is simply not so. They were entirely voluntary bodies started with the full co-operation of, and virtually at the behest of, the trade to act as some sort of protection against what at times seemed like a guerilla action by the protectors of the status quo acting as the informers mentioned.

The results could have been anticipated but were not and, in but a short while, the contradictory judgements of individual Committees matched the contradictions of the Magistrates and found McGill and his managing colleague in the forefront of the pleas for a national censorship to bring some rationality into the affair and to enable trading to go on.

It should soon be possible to have a look at the official papers for the whole period of the 1950s to see whether the Home Secretary did ever have a look at the postcard business. I would think that it is more probable that the 'guerilla action' as I have called it, was genuinely the common informer, with perhaps a nod and a wink between Chief Constables.

Obscenity – The Trials

To relate the story of the trials for publishing obscene matter under the 1857 Act and to quote the cause of the trouble some 30 years after the event is to risk disbelief. I cannot credit that any reader would now contend that anyone, whether young or old, could possibly be corrupted by seeing the cards. Humour, the question of what is or is not funny to each individual, is so unpredictable, even though there are a number of learned and practical books specifying the jokes that always roll them in the aisles. I think the unpredictability comes from a strange process in the brain which is not just waiting to be corrupted or influenced. Looking at a comic card, which is a combination of words and pictures, sets off an active train of thought and associations. However, if there is no personal knowledge of or identification with the situations illustrated then there is no joke. I would contend that the case of the expressed worries of the censor for the influence on the young falls at the first fence. It is only after McGill that the pictures on their own became specifically and patently sexual.

If there is adult comprehension of the subject then the brain will start a series of examinations for acceptability based on all the experiences and influences of the past. Not just the previous influence of other comic cards; but of life as a whole. Perhaps the joke is no joke because it is too uncomfortably true to be accepted. Sometimes self identification leads to release of the tension of secretly held thoughts. The evidence of remarks written on cards actually despatched shows that the comic card says about others what we often think but dare not say.

This apparent diversion when I am relating the story of the trials is only made to clarify the impossible task the law has in dealing with obscenity. Most action was taken under the Obscene Publications Act of 1857; in Hastings the 1885 Improvement Act was used.

The good citizens of Hastings were protected from traders who delivered or exhibited 'for sale or distribution in or near to any street to any inhabitant or passenger any bill or printed or written paper (whether enclosed in a sealed or other envelope, or not) of an obscene or indecent nature, or referring to any disease of a loathsome or secret kind, or to any cure for any such disease, or any profane, indecent, or obscene book, handbill, card, paper, document, print drawing, photograph, painting or representation.'

Grimsby Trial and Others

The brief for the defence of the Cleethorpes shopkeeper appearing at the Grimsby Petty Sessions on the 11 December of 1951, was worth £33 (about £250 in 1983 terms). Add in the costs levied by the Grimsby solicitors and Constance's own London Solicitors and it will be appreciated that several thousands of card sales were absorbed in the exercise. The brief gives backing to my assertion that the common informer was the springboard of Police action, I quote:

'. . . *it is known to the instructing solicitors that pressure was brought upon the Police to pursue this matter by a Magistrate of the same bench who has retired because of her age. She is a woman of very strong temperance and puritanical views and it is understood that she drew attention of the Police to postcards which were being exhibited . . . two other Magistrates authorised the seizure of the cards . . . the Police submitted the cards to the Director of Public Prosecutions, his reply was that some of the cards would not be obscene according to precedential cases . . . however the Police made up their minds that they would not accept responsibility for saying which of the cards seized were and which were not obscene . . .'*

Orders for destruction was made for 13 cards and 51 were cleared for this round of the battle anyway.

In November 1952 Cornwall's premier tobacconist in Newquay wrote to Constance to confirm that the Police were not to appeal against the earlier judgement of the Pydar Magistrates sitting in St Columb who had rejected the claim of Det. Sgt Pope that the McGill cards he had seized were obscene. In 1953 Magistrates at Brighton spent an hour and a quarter poring over 286, or 175 cards, or 300, according to which paper one reads, and rejected 113. Only some of these were McGill's for, as with the Grimsby case, a number of publishers' products were involved; but at that time the Prosecution had not sought to join the suppliers with the hapless retailers. Where appropriate the retailer lost his stock, though certainly Constance at least made this good and the shopkeeper suffered, if that be the word, paying costs of four shillings each (less than £2 today). A quote is of interest, but since it is in only one of the newspaper cuttings to hand I cannot confirm its authenticity!

'You are a sort of Arts Council in this matter,' Mr H. Settegast for two of the owners told the Bench, 'When the Obscene Publications Act 1857 was passed standards of morality were probably lower than today.'

I can only comment, 'Collapse of Stout Party!!'

During this trial and in others the Defence brought the example of Chaucer and Shakespeare to witness, and ever since I do not know anyone who has failed so to do, including me. A final quote from the Defence and with the caveat about reporting, the Prosecution seems to have said nothing at Brighton. A Defence statement was made: 'If you remove the innuendo, there is nothing offensive in the actual illustrations. My clients are doing what shopkeepers are doing in all seaside towns. The cards are vulgar; but not a hidden mischief or obscene.'

We are in the period when it was still, on occasion, necessary for the *Daily Mirror* to speak out in defence of their strip cartoon, for indeed, Jane was most noted for stripping, often enough in far different circumstances from those where the McGillian rationale for nudity was confined to Nudist Camps.

One of the many letters which were written under the signature of Ernest Maidment, even before Ascher's death, requested particulars of a rumoured Censorship Committee. It was referred from Hastings Town Hall to the Police. In 1954 a Committee was set up and was armed by Constance with every card in print and even a note of rejections by the Isle of Man for guidance. In between these dates a further enquiry addressed to the Chief Constable yielded what I must now regard as the definitive attitude of the Police, 1 June 1953.

> '*You wrote on the 27 May asking if there was censorship for cards in Hastings. There is no form of censorship at all. I am not prepared to peruse cards — that is a matter for the court on prosecution being presented. The best thing is for the shopkeepers to use their own common sense, and surely in the event of any question arising in the retailer's mind it is better that he does not handle that line than run the risk of prosecution.*'

The Lincoln Trial, 1954

It was in 1954 that the big guns came out to attack what would now seem to most people in the 1980s some pretty mild 'obscenity', though that was the word used by the anti-postcard faction. The publishers and their representatives would occasionally concede the term 'vulgar' to apply to the product. I find relatively few links to books and pornography. I do not think the term soft or hard as applied to porn had been thought of then. It is indeed somewhat strange that the links were not made more firmly between magazines, books and cards; but again it must be concluded that generally the comic card was available for only the short summer season in coastal areas (though Woolworths did stock them), whereas the worries with regard to pornography or other signs of a new Sodom were city based, and open to attention 365 days of the year.

Examining the firm's correspondence one can only feel sorry for McGill and his management colleague, since on Ascher's death, they had total immediate control of the whole business with worries other than the matter of censorship. It does seem hard that in spite of earnest and genuine efforts to encourage the voluntary controls they still found themselves in the forefront of what may be regarded as the penultimate 'Show Trial' for their product.

It had always been contended that it was publishers other than Constance who were giving the trade a bad name. Judgement as to which publisher had more or less of McGill's 'strong' category jokes seems arbitrary. He admitted to grades starting at mild, then medium and finally strong, though it was denied that such was ever the basis for sales. Which was cruder, which was or was not obscene is very much a matter of individual subjective judgement. The trial at Lincoln Quarter Sessions was society's method of trying to find answers to these questions, or perhaps it was simply trying to interpret the law as it was and to make a judgement within the ethos of the time.

Preparation for trial is a long and tortuous process. The taking of statements by Police and solicitors, the issuing of statutory notices and warnings will all dictate the success or failure of prosecution and defence. This was the trial in which shopkeepers and retailers were joined by the publishers. Victor Durand was briefed for McGill and was armed with life histories and well informed on the contortions of postcard censorship and the cases heard previously.

There was a hearing at the Grimsby County Magistrates Courtroom, 14 April 1954, and under the Royal Coat of Arms 'Honi soit qui mal y pense' judgements were handed out. One company was found not guilty as it seems that one copy only of the one design brought to court could be found anywhere. Easton Millar and its directors were fined on the spot. Constance and its directors joined Bamforth and others in being committed to Lindsey Quarter Sessions in the following July.

In between the two hearings a Police Sergeant Ogilvie paid a visit to the Streatham office, seemingly to confirm addresses and particulars. It would be reasonable to assume that he also took the opportunity to observe whatever was to be observed and pass back information to his country cousins. McGill reported this to his solicitor; but in his usual kindly and considerate way was at pains to say just how polite the sergeant had been.

Times and customs change; but in 1954 at The Castle, Lincoln, McGill and his partner were conducted to the cells, an hour early to await the call for the trial.

A plea of guilty was entered on four counts and resulted in a fine of £50 and costs of £25. (Say, £350 + £175 in today's terms.) Mr Durand's fees for the day totalled the equivalent of £700; this is later recorded as being reduced, but when the Magistrates' Court costs and the retained solicitor's fees are added, considerably in excess of the equivalent of £1,000 was dissipated on this case.

It is not unusual for Counsel to be blamed for court decisions and I suppose that in this case a plea of guilty reinforces such blame; but the defence on any question of obscenity, or more broadly on questions of good and bad taste, were fighting a hard battle in the atmosphere of the 1950s, not the least of their difficulties being their own prejudices. Looking at some of the designs on which Mr Durand was prepared to concede, I am puzzled whether he used his own judgement or his assessment of what a judge might decide. He could not know that the following year the Recorder at Margate would over-rule a Magistrate's condemnation of some very similar cards to those conceded as obscene.

Skirmishes with the law continued and Constance dealt with the complication of the different likes and dislikes of each town censoring body, though in fact this was not so very different from normal variation in demands from region to region experienced by any national distributor. By 1954, trade organised examining bodies for cards were in being, in Blackpool, Hastings, Cleethorpes and Brighton. The retailers in general were naturally somewhat cautious in their buying. Seaside towns are tight little communities and a word of disapproval voiced by a resident would have to be balanced against the comment of a grockle (visitor) and the click of the till. (My very conservative estimate of 10,000 card sales per season would represent £250 plus, profit at today's prices.)

The significance of the Folkestone trial of 1957 is that the Director of Public Prosecutions had become involved. Starting from a 'little local difficulty' it ended in the Recorder at the Maidstone Assizes making a judgement which can only be described as further muddying the waters as to what was and was not obscene. It is not recorded that McGill appeared at these hearings; but the image of both he and Mr Maidment being 'invited to Scotland Yard to assist the police with their enquiries' in connection with the case is to me both a vindication and a condemnation of the legal system in England.

My postcript to this affair has to be a sad one. It would be foolish to claim that McGill never went over that fine line between good and bad taste. The fact that other publishers were prepared to push on that line for selling and competition was at the base of it all. What is puzzling is that the ultimate, if not the immediate, effect of censorship and court proceedings was to put the greatest pressure on those least deserving of condemnation. McGill's work by reason of his vast and long-term output was quite often targeted, together with that of Bamforth. These were 'names' at the front of all reporting. Censoring committees faded and finally ceased operation by the mid 1960s.

The disappearance of McGill from sale is only partially attributable to the above events; but the inability to differentiate between the amusing as opposed to the prurient then, as now, has set the standard for a product today which I find to be distasteful. Some of today's designs would have had no place in the World of Donald McGill.

8
Today-McGill Lives!

Donald Fraser Gould McGill, prolific master of the saucy postcard, died at 87, on 13 October 1962 at St James' Hospital, Balham, London. It would be attractive to think, after all the millions of jokes he was responsible for, that he died of laughing but his death certificate bears witness to more prosaic causes – a gastric ulcer and diverticulutis. He was buried in Streatham Park cemetery, leaving 200 unfinished sketches and his postcard designs for the following season already complete. They were ready and waiting to cheer up any stranded holidaymakers, from Llandudno to Land's End, Bridlington to Blackpool, and to bring them a touch of tittering gaiety to brighten even the dreariest of bank holidays.

McGill's younger daughter thought he should have become a teacher, his older daughter a politician – fortunately for us he became neither. Constance Ltd exported his cards all over the world, to countries without first-hand experience of the British bank holiday and with tastes as disparate as Australia and India. The humour of the 'little man' and the vagaries of sex and marriage appear to have greater universal appeal than one might expect. In 1973 Michael

Tickner produced 'The World of Donald McGill' in Audioscope – a subtle blend of dialogue, sound, music and still pictures. Who would have thought the sophisticated French would have fallen for McGill's naively provocative girls, naughty old men, terrifying mothers-in-law and precocious children? In fact, the French version 'Le Monde Drolatique de Donald McGill' not only had them splitting their sides with laughter but the show earned Michael Tickner the coveted silver cup awarded at the 13th International Festival de L'Image held at Epinal in the Vosges. The fact that McGill's cards had this wide appeal and were reproduced in their millions, led to the assumption, often repeated in newspapers, that he made a fortune out of his work. This became a popular myth; in fact he proved to be far less of a canny Scot than the hundreds he portrayed. It is not even an ironic joke that when McGill died in 1962 his estate was valued at only £735 – little more than would be paid today for a handful of his best originals. The man who profited from his efforts, died in 1951, then nominally worth £40,000. The quoted figures for an estate may often conceal more than they reveal but the figures do have some significance. After McGill's death, there was no safe deposit box to find or notes stuffed into shoe boxes, no chaos, no difficulties left behind. Here was a man who worked to maintain his family and live an

196

honourable life. He made his will in his own elegant hand and most of the resources he left must have been due to his later earnings, 'under contract' rather than from the work which spanned his lifetime and included his most productive periods. During the First World War 18 million of his cards were sold. He recalled the days when 'the soppy stuff went down like mother's milk'. The Second World War found us less sentimental and whilst Hitler's bombs could not diminish McGill's irrepressible mirth, German torpedoes severed the supply of the basic raw materials from which postcards were made. Although he was 70 by the end of that war McGill went on producing laughter through the 'New McGill Comics'. Following Ascher's death his contract was to produce 36 sketches each half year! A remarkable feat for a man in his late 70s. Some he would complete in a few hours – others he would wrestle with for weeks.

He did not approve of anonymity. Not for him the usual postcard artist's pseudonym. He was not ashamed to place his neat, careful signature on his work. In 1957 he offered to give evidence before the House of Commons' Select Committee, which was considering a Bill to amend the outdated 1857 Obscene Publications Act. He wrote a letter of protest to *The Times* against being written off as a syndicate in George Orwell's essay. Nevertheless, despite some inaccuracies and the tendency to over-sentimentalise working class attitudes, Orwell's essay was a seminal influence on the acceptance by the literati of McGill's work as genuine examples of folk art. McGill enjoyed the resultant limelight in his declining years but he was not seduced by it. In fact, when you consider that he found such solace in his library of over 2,000 volumes, there were very few literary jokes apart from the oft quoted query by the bookish young man reading *Kim* to his giggling long-legged miss, 'Do you like Kipling?' and her reply which is a coy invitation, 'I don't know, you naughty boy, I've never kippled!'

Although McGill finally became something of a cult figure he knew his market and he stuck to it; leaving it to others to interpret the significance of his humour and his art.

Orwell pointed out that there is not much room for the humorous view of life in 'codes of law, morals and religious systems. Whatever is funny is subversive, every joke is ultimately a custard pie and the reason why so large a proportion of jokes centre around obscenity is simply that all societies, as the price of survival, have to insist on a fairly high standard of sexual morality.' He saw the dirty joke not as a serious attack upon morality but as 'a sort of mental rebellion, a momentary wish that things were otherwise'. He felt that McGill's jokes were 'like a chorus of raspberries' in the face of pomposity and moralising. They stood for the 'worm's eye view of life'.

'They were meant to be vulgar and ugly. The slightest hint of higher influences would ruin them utterly.' The portrayal of McGill's voluptuous females he saw as 'not intended as pornography, but a subtler thing, as a skit on pornography.' Benny Green sees them as a 'skit on eroticism'. I think that, together with the other McGill archetypes, they are a skit on real life, extracting from it those aspects of birth, courtship, marriage, middle-age and death from which McGill could squeeze a laugh — and exercise his ready wit: for example, there is father at the newspaper office, 'I want you to put this notice of the birth of my son in your paper,' 'Yes sir, how many insertions?' 'Mind your own business!' was the huffy riposte, and the nurse saying to the new Dad, 'Your wife's had triplets!' 'Well I never did!' 'Oh, go on,' she titters 'You must have done!' McGill's own favourite joke is relatively mild with shocked 'nanny' overtones. 'There's the Vicar at the window sponging his Aspidistra,' 'Horrid old man! He ought to do it in the bathroom.' *(Plates 112, 122).*

There was always a 'catch 22' in the condemnation by the pious of the elegant euphemism and the delicate double entendre which McGill wittily displayed. If the moralising critics could understand the jokes, perhaps they were not as pure as they would like to have us believe! Lesser mortals laughed. Gerard Benson writing in the *New Statesman* in 1974 about McGill's work in the exhibition of 'Cartoon Originals' owned by Bernard Levin and Robin Ray said, 'It is a comic simplification of the real world' – and within this seaside world, 'we are allowed again to laugh, as we in childhood laughed, totally committed to the humour of the fat bum.' It is the anarchic quality of McGill's jokes that I find most irresistible: the stern notice in the art gallery demands SILENCE. 'But you can't keep a girl from thinking,' says the toothy matron, admiring the nude male statue of 'The Lover'.

After more than 40 years in the trade, McGill told a reporter in 1948 that it still hurt if someone referred to his work as 'smutty'. For the life of him, he said, he could not see how in the land of Marie Lloyd, George Robey, Nellie Wallace, Max Miller and the not too intellectual double entendre, any picture of his could endanger public taste. To Tom Baistow at the time of the obscenity trials, he stated vehemently in a *News Chronicle* interview in 1957, 'My cards obscene? Nonsense! Of course they're vulgar – but it's honest vulgarity. This is a vulgar age. Look at that £104,000 paid for a Gauguin the other day – that's vulgarity isn't it?'

Has there been indignation in heaven as the price of McGill's originals has steadily increased? Using his yardstick, is ours a more 'vulgar' age than the 1940s?

McGill was not given to artistic pretensions but, later in life, having beaten the panel in the TV programme 'What's my Line?', he was stung into replying, with some dignity, to Gilbert Harding's aggressive, 'So you do those dirty postcards?' with – 'No, I am a seaside artist.'

Attitudes towards McGill as an artist are contradictory. Orwell calls his designs child-like, 'full of heavy lines and empty spaces,' – 'deliberately ugly in hideous colours'. I assume Orwell was not familiar with McGill's best work of the 1920s. Richard Carline in *Pictures in the Post* adopts a somewhat dismissive attitude to McGill's later work suspecting, like Orwell, that it was done by others and applying aesthetic standards which are not entirely appropriate, when one considers that McGill was working for an industry and a market which had its own demands and restraints. As McGill stated, he had to make a living. Carline does make the point though, that if the card characters were more 'realistically' drawn not so many might enjoy them without blushing. Calder-Marshall mentions a more sympathetic appreciation by the late Claude Rogers, former Director of the School of Fine Art, Reading University. He admired McGill's 1920s originals for their mastery of detail and likened some of the drawing to that of McGill's contemporary Fernand

Léger. I think there is also some similarity in the way they both treat bold, flat areas of colour. Certainly they both explored the rich vein of popular art which placed the common man at its centre and which retained a common touch. Calder-Marshall, in his affectionate biography, claims that McGill's world is 'of such obscene vulgarity that it creates its own sub-reality – like Hieronymus Bosch's vision of hell.'

Nearer home one can see in some of Beryl Cook's caricatures and stereotypes possible descendants from the McGill entourage. She also retains the common touch. Like McGill she likes painting people who are enjoying themselves and she too has few artistic pretensions. Her statement that, 'There's nothing profound about my painting,' might have echoed from Bennett Park.

It is surprising how many writers, comedians and artists have retained a soft spot for McGill. Roy Hattersley recently referred to him as 'The Leonardo of the saucy postcard'. Dennis Potter called him the 'Picasso of the Pier' and the 'Munnings of Margate'. Rupert Besley acknowledges that in McGill's 'drawing style and handling of paint there is an affectionate warmth and sensitivity that sets him poles apart from today's cheap imitations.' His work appeals to tastes as divergent as those of Bernard Levin, Auberon Waugh, John Osborne, Larry, (Terence Parkes the cartoonist), Robin Ray, Ronnie

Barker, Bob Monkhouse, Ian Hamilton Finlay and the late Kenneth More. For the latter, the artist Leslie Coleman, also a McGill collector and enthusiast, created a brilliant mural, a pastiche of McGill's fat lady looking surprised through a simulated hole in the wall, cunningly made by the splashing briny. It is a mural which brings the seaside right into the sitting room – as McGill's cards did. Leslie Coleman has also produced four large pastiches of McGill's work for Reeves which make up part of a painting course for adults.

Far less faithful imitations and plagiarisms occur with astonishing frequency in the advertising world. McGill's work is reproduced or his style is simulated because he now represents part of the 'British way of life' and his art is therefore considered appropriate to highlight typically British products like Bemax and a brand of ubiquitous brown sauce.

His work was even used as a recruiting poster for the Australian Air Force! The British Travel Association and others have enquired but have drawn back – too naughty?

Despite many imitations, a McGill original is easily recognisable by its style and by the caption written on the reverse side of each painting, together with the instructions for the blockmakers and printers. Sometimes, last minute or alternative captions were inscribed with one or more reference numbers. The numbers, however, bear little relationship to those issued on the final cards. Unhappily, McGill only dated some of the early work and some of the original designs were never used as cards. If Ascher did not receive enough orders for the following summer season from the originals, he would not go to the expense of making blocks. There are a number of unsigned originals which are unquestionably McGill's work and which can be easily identified by the graceful and distinctive handwriting on the back.

The main cache of originals resulted from two sales made by D. Constance Ltd through Sotheby's in 1967 and 1968. A total of about 2,000 paintings were sold (without copyright) for £2,400, but prices have risen steadily since then. Sanders of Oxford were the enterprising major purchasers and McGill could not have wished for a better re-distributor of his work, which is now spread widely. These originals turn up at major and minor sales and, much in the manner of antiques, seem to pass from dealer to dealer before disappearing into a collector's home.

Present day prices are so variable that figures do not have a great deal of significance. The market responds to whim and fashion, but a little persistence might enable a collector to pick up a reasonable example for £20-£30. However, where the subject has a special appeal, such as the many happy boozers, which are relevant and attractive to the licensed trade, then £100-£150 would not be untoward.

I have come to suspect that amongst the Sotheby's sales there may have been some of the earlier pre-Second World War originals which somehow survived the bombing of Ivy Lane but it would take considerable further research to track down each original and relate it to subsequent cards. To add to the confusion, post-marks of the relevant cards do not necessarily relate to the date of printing, nor does the date of printing relate to the date of the creation of the original.

Since the paintings were essentially for commercial reproduction and since many were dated quickly by events, a number would no doubt be cast aside, after one or more runs, and even the plates returned for scrap. When my husband and his friend, Michael Tickner, bought the remaining stocks from D. Constance Ltd in 1972, there were included in the package, a number of three colour plates which have been preserved, even though they may never again be placed on a printing machine.

Many of the surviving artist's originals now find themselves as part of an art market where they are amongst some very strange bedfellows. I had always hoped that in an attic somewhere would be found a hoard of McGill's paintings ranging over the first 25 years, though I had begun to think this unlikely. However in 1982 some pre-1939 Inter-Art originals appeared on the market and were sold for a good price by Stanley Gibbons. I would not be surprised now if even earlier originals surfaced. They too will inevitably attract high prices and, more importantly perhaps, will illustrate that the man who devoted a life-time to the comic postcard was a watercolourist of some stature, whose later work did not always do his talent justice.

For anyone interested in purchasing or selling originals, contact should made with the main salerooms such as Sotheby's, Christie's, Gibbons' and Phillip's, and an inquiry to Sanders of Oxford with regard to their present stock might well prove fruitful.

McGill's work, both originals and cards, may appear also in smaller salerooms up and down the country, such as the Garnet Langton Auctions in Bournemouth. They are often put up for sale under different headings and may appear under 'Fine Art' or 'Memorabilia'. Sometimes one finds mixed parcels of cards mounted and unmounted and, very occasionally, originals at the numerous postcard fairs. Prior notice of these may be culled from a perusal of the pages of postcard magazines such as *Picture Postcard Monthly* – a magazine which can be recommended for anyone seeking good background to the postcard world. The magazine *Stamp News and Postal History*, the official journal of the British

Philatelic Federation Ltd, also has a useful postcard section. Contact with the Postcard Club of Great Britain may well be fruitful.

Just as attitudes to McGill as an artist may be seen to be contradictory so may the attitudes of the collector compared with the attitudes of the general public. The serious collector is a breed apart, varying from the highly specialised, extremely knowledgeable, to the man playing 'the numbers game' and rather more interested in completing the 'set' than what is actually in it. With a few notable exceptions the 'serious' postcard collector is more interested in pre 'New McGills' than in the later output, probably because the range of the latter is so wide and the supply plentiful. Though it might take some time to assemble a complete set of 'New McGill's' it is certainly within the range of possibility to do so. As with originals, quotations for prices of cards can be somewhat deceiving but Brian Lund, the editor of *Picture Postcard Monthly*, quoted the following guidelines in August 1983: 80p for early ones (1911-1918), 50p for 1919-1939, and 15p for the final period – for single buys. The majority, however, may well change hands as part of comprehensive collections, where the time and place of sale may have more to do with the price realised than the age or condition of the items.

Donald McGill's figures given in reply to

journalists enquiring about the actual number of designs he had executed were 10,000 in 1949 and 12,000 by 1957. These figures were at one time written off as exaggerations but more recent research shows that 10,000 plus is not unlikely. Mr Robert Scott the premier collector has '8,483 cards excluding reprints, re-issues and duplicated publications'! Mr Ray Collier, a specialist collector of Inter-Art Co. cards can list approximately 3,600 of McGill's designs.

In his excellent book *Collecting Picture Postcards* Anthony Byatt lists no less than 80 comic postcard artists. Of these it is noteworthy that the mythical man-in-the-street, not to be confused with the legendary postcard collector, would recognise only a handful of artists of any sort and only one as a postcard artist. McGill is like Nescafé, a known brand name used and confused. The phenomenon may well be explained simply by the volume and the extended period of his output. The public of all ages and people of 40 plus who were buyers of McGill when he stood boldly in the racks, join in seeing him essentially as the 'Fat Lady Man'. There must be literally thousands of homes where a few McGills rest in the back of a drawer. They are known to be there and are never discarded – an aide-memoire of the past.

The under 40s will be happy to buy a few cards just

"And the next time you sew a button on the master's trousers—wait till he takes them off!"

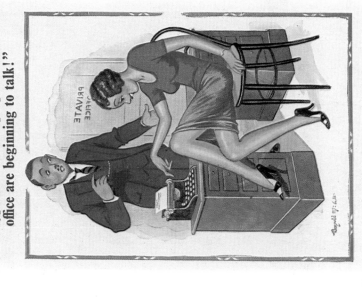

"You really must learn to use the typewriter. The people in the office are beginning to talk!"

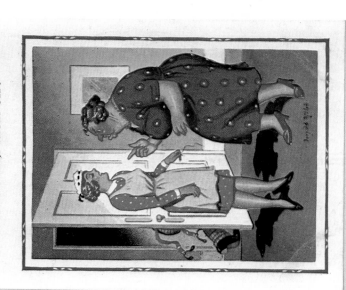

"I was only a slip of a girl when we were married!"
"Well, blimey, you've slipped a bit since!!"

Old or young, tall or short,
Pick 'em out at random.
This bally town seems full of men
Whose wives don't understand 'em!

"But we **must** keep having 'em. My wife's Maternity Benefit is the only income I've got!"

"Your husband on the dole again! Isn't there *anything* he sticks at regularly?"

"That was a splendid sermon you gave about the 'Foolish Virgins,' Vicar. I'll never be one again!"

"Oh, my dear Curate, we didn't know what Sin was in our village until you came!"

"You surely admit the existence of a
    supreme and all powerful will?"
"Certainly, I do! I married it!!"

"Do you know who I am?"
"Of course, I do. I married
    your sister!"

"Brassiere? Yes, Madam; what bust?"
"Ee luv, nothing bust, it just wore out!"

"Gentlemen's Requisites? Yes, Sir, go right through 'Ladies' Underwear'!"

"All you want, you know, is a little sun and air."

'Oh, Doctor, you naughty man! At my time of life!!"

"Oh, Painter, I want you to touch up the place where my husband put his hand last night!"

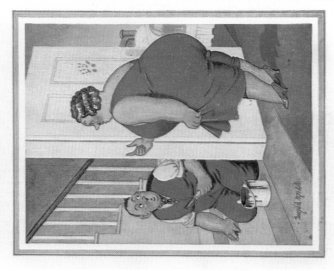

"There's the Vicar at the window
sponging his Aspidistra."
"Horrid old man! He ought to do
it in the Bathroom!"

Can't see you to-night---
I'm washing my hair

Mummy, did you find baby under the
Gooseberry bush?

Yes dear.

Well, he's got a thorn sticking in him.

"Putting on weight, ain't
you, Mrs. Ramsbottom?"

"Don't be silly, Bert, here's someone coming!"

" Censor or no Censor, I've got to hold my hat on!"

"I should like a swim, but I don't want to get my truncheon wet!"

A Stick of Rock, Cock?

"She's a nice girl. Doesn't drink or smoke, and only swears when it slips out!"

"Take this jelly away, Waiter. There are TWO things on this earth that I like firm and ONE of them's jelly!"

"What, twins again, Mrs. Lovejoy! Do
you always have twins?"
"Oh no, Vicar! Lots of times we don't
have anything at all!!"

"Your wife's had triplets!"
"Well, I never did!"
"Oh, go on, you must have done!!"

"You know, Dear, it's the *wives* of these strikers that I'm sorry for!"

"I say, Milkman, have you the time?"
"Yes, I've the *time*, but 'oo's going to look after my 'orse?"

"But surely, Darling, you're not going to bed in that thing on our Honeymoon?"
"Well, Dearest, Mother told me that if I was a sensible girl I should take precautions!"

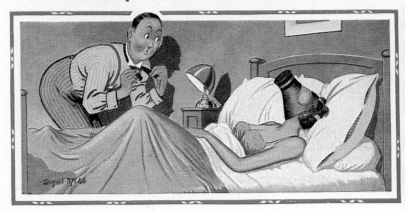

"Good Heavens! I dreamt I was married!!"

because they have heard about McGill on TV or radio or they have read about him 'somewhere or the other'. Joseph Ascher had the sense to use his artist as a brand name by cleverly giving the artist's work an individuality and labelling cards clearly, 'The New McGill Series'. It is a chastening thought that the artists Tempest and Taylor of Bamforth & Co. are rarely mentioned by the man-in-the-street and yet their publisher would claim a greater output than McGill for each of them. Mr Taylor, being a director of Bamforth & Co., should perhaps have proposed his own elevation to a brand name!

Whether media coverage was the greatest factor in keeping McGill's name in the forefront is difficult to assess. Certainly, the centenary of his birth in 1975 resulted in his exposure to the combined circulations of such diverse publications as the *Observer, Radio Times,* the *Sun,* the *Nursing Mirror* and *The Times Business News!* More recently he has been featured in various magazines and national newspapers. One can confidently expect to find some direct or oblique reference to McGill appearing in the press practically every month! Certainly Orwell's essay has been influential. I would like to think it has been read in its entirety as often as parts of it have been quoted.

The newsworthy obscenity trials often gave a quite unwelcome spurt to McGill's publicity. The glorious contradiction of a gentle and kindly old man being a source of naughtiness was just too good to resist. Having now read many articles written about the man, I would urge anyone aiming to be famous, that they should ensure that the very first mention of them in press, TV or radio is true and accurate, for if the alleged facts get on to a file, they appear to become 'the facts', right or wrong.

It is now more than 20 years since McGill sat with his child's metal paint box to create one more design. The colour wash drawing was intended primarily to be reproduced as a postcard to a size virtually unchanged in the six decades in which he applied himself to the job. McGill is unique. Apart from a few Valentine broadsheets he confined his original designs to a format which was twice the size of the final product. That area must have been as familiar to him as the lined confines of a court to a tennis star.

The layout, the colour contrasts, the content were specifically commercially dictated and I think explains the affinity of present day commercial artists to his work. The creative 'one-off' painter will choose board or canvas to suit the subject he has in mind; he has little concern with the reproduction processes which might follow or, by and large, that there should be mass-appeal in his work. Most wielders of the brush are not in it for the money anyway and those who earn a living by it can grant themselves the indulgence of changes in size and presentation which are totally denied to a postcard creator.

Some of McGill's admirers have the discipline of the confines of a four column spread in their productions for commerce and advertising. They have said to me that they would have been driven mad to have always had to face one area to fill with their brush.

It has been the purpose of this book to set McGill in context within the world of postcards and most particularly that part of this world which he truly dominated. There were better artists, probably better humorists in the field. In the case of the former, it has been stated that McGill's work was not primarily an artistic effort to be looked at and examined for its line and brush strokes. As far as humour is concerned it would be a bold man who claims the creation of an original joke; certainly McGill always gave us that slight new twist that makes the old seem new.

Looking around the comic card racks today much of the work seems distasteful. The subtle double entendre, the innocuous and gentle innuendo seem not to exist. The crudity of the sexual jokes and drawings finds only the rarest of parallels in McGill. Perhaps the point of satiation has arrived? As an experiment and with the co-operation of a seafront shop proprietor, a number of McGill's 'old-fashioned' designs were displayed with current stock. To my surprise they were joyously snapped up!

227

Happily I found one artist, Rupert Besley, whose humour shows some affinity with the teasing, twinkle of McGill. His cards are published by J. Arthur Dixon of the Isle of Wight. Their more usual field is the greetings card, though they have produced views for many years and are gently 'feeling the water' for a new seaside product, conforming to their other high quality output. One can only wish them and their cartoonist a good response from the buying public.

Rupert Besley generously writes of McGill – 'whether or not we realise it, a great many of us, scrawlers and salesmen, owe our livelihoods to McGill for making the seaside postcard an indispensable national institution. Of course there were others at work with him in the same area, but for me, only McGill passes the tests that make his work truly classic: he captured situations of universal appeal and, above all, he produced cartoons that are just as funny today as they were the day they were drawn. Not many people manage that.'

The events of yesterday make up today's nostalgia. Looking through McGill's cards now, they have a period charm and one can see why they have become part of the nostalgia boom. No doubt the day before yesterday has always seemed more attractive than the immediate present. How else can one explain the popularity of 'The Good Old Days', said to be the longest running TV show in the world! Started in

1953 it aimed to re-create the hey-day of Mr Hurley's Victorian Music Hall. The large London hotels are now offering their svelte clientele tea dances à la 20s and cocktails. Harrod's catalogue this season contains an advertisement for Harem trousers – shades of 1912! Leslie Ash recently appeared in the TV show 'Give us a Clue' attired in a pastel striped suit which owed a lot to the old cover-all Victorian bathing dress – the caleçon.

After the surfeit of nudism and topless beaches, the residents of Cleethorpes found a wet T-Shirt competition quite popular this summer. No doubt the titillation by imitation of the clinging qualities of the old flannel swim suit had their 'novel' appeal. There are moves afoot to restore the old fashioned bathing huts and to save the Victorian piers in places like Clevedon and Swanage. Southend, the largest pier of the lot, is to receive £1 million for restoration, and the Palace Pier at Brighton has sported a National Museum of Penny Slot Machines. John Hayward, the director calls it 'An Edwardian Palace of Amusement' where once again you can see 'What the Butler Saw' and '100 Vintage Exhibits of Seaside Fun'.

During the summer of 1983 a nostalgic exhibition and museum called 'Remember When?' was mounted on Hastings Pier, by John Henty, freelance journalist and broadcaster. As well as being able to buy old pennies to work the amusement machines and mechanical music-makers, one could follow the vagaries of seaside humour from Edwardian times to the 1960s through an exhibition of McGill's cards. Art students decorated part of the exhibition area with a McGill style mural. Appropriately enough, the exhibition was at the end of the pier, opposite the pub and next to the ladies toilet! It was an extremely imaginative show. With such renewed public interest in nostalgia would it be too fanciful now to envisage Larry's cartoon of a McGill retrospective really coming to life? Is there a prestigious gallery that would risk it?

There is an implication that the world of Donald McGill died with his passing in 1962. The total cut-off in the supply of his cards to the trade was in 1972 or even earlier, as Constance abandoned efforts to market what they saw as out-dated products. Certainly the retail supply of cards died but not his world. He cemented the long tradition of bawdy, vulgar, British jokes which have raised a guffaw or a giggle from the time of the Canterbury Tales to the most modern pantomine. Master of the genre of the saucy postcard, his prodigious output has been hailed as being as British as fish and chips, stout and winkles, buckets and spades, seaside rock and sad-eyed donkeys – his humour as heady as the froth blown from a pint at the end of the pier – and it has been called 'the stuff that won two world wars'. After the sale in January 1983 of some of his originals the *Daily Mail* leader-writer said, 'Let the connoisseurs at Christie's admire his brush work, the rest of us salute the supreme exponent of the belly laugh!' His were time-honoured themes – the humour of the chamber pot, the pulchritudinous chamber maid, the eager old maid, the flighty flirt, the suave seducer, the final surrender and the bungled honeymoon.

Marital bliss becomes the battle of the sexes, and genial alcoholism, bodily functions and impertinent children keep us laughing. His gallery was joined by nudists, Scots, vicars and tradesmen with their malapropisms, their innuendoes and their awful puns in the best British music hall tradition. His is the humour of the playground, the pub, the rugby club and the work's outing.

There is a modern myth that we all go abroad for our holidays. According to the British Tourist Authority which defines a holiday as 'four nights or more away from home,' 41% of the population in 1982 had no holiday. Many had to be content with only a weekend or a day trip by the sea. Go to any seaside town though and study what happens after the coaches disgorge their passengers. Within half-an-hour many of them can be seen scribbling postcards, stalking round to find the Post Office or welcome red pillar-box – sending their saucy 'wish you were here' messages − urgent proof that they made it to places like Blackpool, Bournemouth and Bridlington. Hundreds of harmless, trite messages are scrawled to people like the tea lady, uncle George, auntie Gwen and grandma Louie on their preferred list, and blatantly rude missives to those left behind in office or factory who may be on their hit list.

It will not be long before the fat bathers on the beach catch the eye. The women may be better fed, better housed, better clothed and more figure conscious than their predecessors but there still seem to be plenty of fat men around. If the women are no longer obese from constant childbearing, the men, judging from many of their vanished waist-lines, are still merrily boozing. McGill's coquettish flappers have been replaced by today's dolly-birds, the knuts and the mashers by today's super-studs. They are still seeking each other out − still flirting. The promenade is still the arena for early coquetry and later groping. The little perishers, gorged on candy floss and chips, still wreak havoc in the amusement arcade and on dad's pocket. The holiday spent with food from a take-away in a holiday flat is but a step from the furnished apartments on offer in the 1930s at Clacton or Bognor, where mother carried out her task of buying food to be cooked by madame.

From the security of his seat in heaven − atheist or not − no doubt dear Donald is thinking up jokes on the far from luxury flats which will greet the unwary. My impression is that many modern comic card artists have considerable difficulty in forgetting the area below the waist line. I am convinced that Donald would have rung the changes with jokes about the vast number of pensioners who now invade resorts in and out of season. He could not have resisted the contradiction of the Brits eating Greek, Indian and Chinese take-aways; TV's in tents, the ubiquitous jeans and Walkman stereos. In addition, many of his old favourite characters are still around. Womens' Lib may have done marvels for women but some claim that it has added to the number of hen-pecked men! Both groups would have received his attention! It can be seen that the exuberant, colourful world of Donald McGill is still very much alive.

Few will go and gaze at the blue plaque in Bennett Park but thousands will remember the broken red or blue border round McGill's cards and, despite the transitory quality of the comic card, they will remember the seaside he created and his jokes. Apparently secret longings for nifty buttocks, large boobs and virile men die hard.

Above the thousands of cards in his sales office hung a text, 'Let us endeavour so to live that when we come to die, even the undertaker will be sorry'. A biographer, I think, can say no better of any human being than that after viewing his life and work the final conclusion must be that here was a very good and honourable man who left this world with the happiest of memories for all who knew him.

But to Donald Fraser Gould McGill must go the last laugh. After more than 60 years of gleeful creativity he announced 'I never go to the seaside – and I never send people cards!'

Appendix-An Outline of Postcard History

It is to the USA that we must look for the distinction of being the country where the world's first postcard appeared. It was a private card for which in 1861, Mr John P. Charlton of Philadelphia held the copyright. This he later transferred to a fellow Philadelphian Mr H. Lipman, who was responsible for printing and selling 'Lipman's Postal Cards' which were quite plain. There are only four of the original printing known in existence. The second issue had a red, blue or green scroll border, lines on one side for the address and a plain back to carry the maximum message. The United States Postal Act of 1861 approved their use and fixed them with a one cent stamp rate. They were used until the US Government issued their own official cards in 1873.

Meanwhile, Europe was moving towards a cheaper, easier and less formal means of communication than the letter. Some postcards (charged at letter rate and with small pictures or decorations down one side) had already appeared for business purposes in France and North Germany. Subsequently, at an Austro-German postal conference in Karlsruhe in 1865, Dr Heinrich von Stephan suggested using an open post-sheet – an

'Offenes Postblatt' of envelope size with a space on the left for a date stamp and on the right for an impressed postage stamp. Below was to be the addressee's name and address and the reverse side would have the maximum space for a message from travellers and tradesmen. It was thought this idea might decrease post office revenue and nothing was done about it until Dr Emmanuel Herrmann wrote to Vienna's *Nieue Frie Press* in January 1869 suggesting a 'new' method of correspondence by post — 'by the use of plain cards, envelope size, with an imprinted two Kreuzer stamp on the same side as the address and a message not exceeding twenty words on the reverse side.' By 1 October, 1869, the idea had been adopted with no restriction on the number of words in the Austro-Hungarian Empire and in the first year nearly a million of the new 'Correspondenz-Karte' were sold each month, to be swiftly followed by illustrated cards. Cards were even dropped from balloons during the siege of Paris 1870-71.

In the British Isles there was the same opposition to the use of a plain card. In Victorian times many of the educated minority valued the art of letter writing as evidence of a cultured mind. There were certain formalities, euphemisms and circumlocution which it was expected the well-bred writer would observe. The idea of sending a message necessarily abbreviated and at cheap rate, open to all who handled it, was quite offensive to some. Others believed that people might be openly libelled. Nevertheless, with Gladstone's encouragement, Dr Lyon Playfair led a successful campaign for a card post and the first official plain postcard, for inland use only, coincided with the first day of issue of the half-penny postage stamp on 1 October 1870. It was a thin buff card 4.8in×3.5in (122 mm×88 mm), modified six weeks later to 4.8in×2.9in (121 mm×74 mm) with an imprinted stamp of Queen Victoria, a small print of the royal coat of arms and a border of geometrical design in purple. It carried the words: POSTCARD – THE ADDRESS ONLY TO BE WRITTEN THIS SIDE. TO – and was printed by Thomas de la Rue & Co Ltd. The age of the brief message in Britain had begun. These cards were sold for a half-penny, the price of the stamp, 575,000 of them on the first day, though stationers agitated against the injustice of the de la Rue monopoly. From 17 July 1872, anyone could print plain cards as near as possible to the size of the official card, but they still had to have the stamp impressed or imprinted by the Inland Revenue. Mr Gladstone who became a great postcard user proposed that a better quality white card should be introduced and this was done in 1875.

The year that McGill was born, 1875, saw an important international development. It became possible to send cards abroad. The US Postmaster

General, Montgomery Blair, had foreseen the need to simplify the postage rates for mail travelling between countries. These differed according to weight and route. He instigated an international conference in Paris as early as May 1863, but progress was delayed by the American Civil War and the Franco-Prussian War. However, the idea was taken up again after Blair's retirement by Heinrich von Stephan. At an international conference at Berne, Switzerland in 1874, 22 countries formed the General Postal Union, later to become the Universal Postal Union. Agreement was reached on 1 July, 1875 that letter rate would be 2½d per half ounce for member countries and a postcard could be sent for half this rate. By 1878, the cost for a card was reduced to 1d for countries whose letter rate was 2½d and 1½d for those where the letter rate was 4d. The first cards headed Union Postale Universelle Great Britain brought forth such a storm of protest from Ireland that a new issue was quickly printed with the words 'Postcard Great Britain & Ireland'. In the early 1870s, many European countries issued cards, and Russia and Canada by 1872. By 1873, they were issued for 'the requirements of business and social life' in the USA. From the beginning, greetings and advertisements were printed on the back. On the first day of issue of cards in London in 1870 the Royal Polytechnic Institute of Regent Street sent a card to its patrons advertising its programme of entertainments and welcoming the introduction of the half-penny postage.

Exhibitions acted as a great spur to the postcard industry. Special advertising cards were available at the International Industrial Exhibition in Chicago (1873) and in Cincinnati (1874). In England, the Great Exhibition of 1851 was followed by one in 1862 where a full postal service was offered. A whole series of special exhibitions followed and were so significant that the National Postal Museum has held (6 January – 1 July 1983) an exhibition about exhibitions from 1851-1951!

Rowland Hill received some late recognition in the summer of 1890 when cards were issued for the Golden Jubilee of the Penny Post. Underneath his portrait are the words, 'He gave us penny postage'. The card was issued to be enclosed in its accompanying envelope which bore the royal monogram and imprinted one penny stamp. A postman 1840s style is on one side and 1890s style on the other. Progress during the intervening years is shown by the North Mail coach, making for Highgate at 8 mph and below the North Mail train making for Carlisle at the then great speed of 48 mph. As with the Mulready envelopes, caricatures soon appeared.

A real breakthrough towards the increased popularity of the postcard had been made in the previous year at the Paris Exhibition held in 1889. The Eiffel Tower, the world's highest man-made structure at that time, was a central feature and it was possible to buy a card with a lithographed picture of the tower, on the left of the message side, mark it with a cross and post it from the top. The idea proved to be a great success and X marks the spot on hundreds of later picture postcards of promontory, mountain, cliff or humble hotel room. Although the top section of the Eiffel Tower was closed when I visited it at Easter 1983, tourists were still gathering in great numbers to post their cards from the second platform.

The origin of the idea was copied at the Royal Naval Exhibition in 1891 and The Gardening and Forestry Exhibition at Earls Court in 1893, when cards could be posted from the top of a model of the Eddystone Lighthouse!

By the 1890s Germany, Austria and Switzerland were way ahead of Britain and the USA in the production of pictorial view-cards. The simple expedient of printing 'Greetings from', 'Gruss Aus' or 'Souvenir de' gave the traveller the cachêt he needed to impress his friends back home. Since at this stage no message could be written on the address side of cards, small multiple views were arranged on the other side with some space left for a greeting. Famous views, buildings, hotels and monuments were shown, often linked with scrolls and flowers. Many were printed in Germany by collotype and later chromo-lithography. The effect of some of these early 'Gruss Aus' cards was quite beautiful and one can understand why they became so popular. By the end of the century souvenir cards were being printed for places all over the world – Buddha's image for sale in Rangoon was printed in Germany – the Pyramids of Egypt in France, views of New Zealand actually printed in London. In the USA their first picture postcards, as distinct from advertising cards, were on sale at the World Columbian Exhibition at Chicago in May 1893. Travellers abroad could buy their picture postcards in shops, hotels, railway stations and restaurants, in fact every journey was punctuated by the selling, buying and writing of cards. It was referred to as the 'German plague'. The influx of picture postcards from Europe led to great agitation on the part of English publishers and stationers. Their efforts were backed by Mr Henniker-Heaton, MP and the restrictions were finally lifted here on 1 September 1894. From this date picture postcards could be privately printed, sold everywhere in the British Isles and posted with the half-penny adhesive stamp. However, at this stage, they were only intended for internal use and had to conform to the size of the official card (maximum 4.8in × 2.9in) (122 mm × 75 mm). A more square-shaped card card known as the court card – 4½in × 3½in (115 mm ×

89 mm) had been in use for some time, often printed with small pictures and usually posted in envelopes. By 1895, it was permitted to post the court cards on their own and an intermediate size 5.1in × 3.3in (130 mm × 83 mm) followed. Pictorial view cards began to appear in every town and city, led by the firm of George Stewart of Edinburgh who had previously published pictorial notepaper. Other companies followed, including another Scotch firm James Valentine of Dundee, producing collotype views from 1895. Some of the early work is fine, often combining collotype, chromo-lithography and embossing. Cards featuring topical events and personalities followed. Queen Victoria's Diamond Jubilee in 1897 furthered the trend to produce 'Royalty' cards. The best of the British cards rivalled those of Germany, but the latter had the advantage of being larger.

Thanks to the efforts of Mr Adolph Tuck, managing director of Raphael Tuck & Sons, the restrictions on the size of British postcards were lifted on 1 November, 1899. The larger size 5½in × 3½in (140 mm × 89 mm) meant that British firms could compete at last on equal terms with European publishers. The fervent patriotism of the Boer War (1899-1902) gave postcards a great boost and those designed by Harry Payne and Richard Caton Woodville became immediately popular.

Firms used the new large postcards for advertisements and sales correspondence, but the public in late Victorian times were upset by the appearance in 1895 of what became known as the 'Beer and Baccy Card'. Printed in Victoria, Australia it had official blessing there as a source of revenue. The penny imprinted stamp of Queen Victoria in the right hand corner shared the space with advertisements on the left for Havelock's aromatic plug tobacco and Foster's Lager Beer. Such exception was taken to this combination that the card had to be withdrawn.

In the United States, advertising cards available from the early 1870s were followed by view cards of every description and on 19 May 1898, Congress followed the British example and authorised the sale of private postcards, which from that time until Christmas Eve 1901 had to carry a Private Mailing Card heading. Pre-1898 view cards in the United States are known as 'Pioneer Postcards' and these are anxiously sought. Some of the earliest 'Gruss Aus' types were produced by a Boston firm the American Souvenir Company as early as 1895. Anthony Byatt in his book *Collecting Picture Postcards* quotes a writer to the Standard in 1899, 'The illustrated postcard craze, like the influenza, has spread to these Islands, from the Continent, where it has been raging with considerable severity.'

By 1900, 419 million postcards on every conceivable subject were posted in Britain and a positive craze for collecting cards – cartomania – had begun. In 1901 the winner of a competition organised by Raphael Tuck had collected over 20,000 of their cards with different postmarks. Cards were retailed for 1d each or even less and since they were printed in sets, this encouraged the collectors. Postcard magazines arrived on the scene and collectors' clubs were established all over the world. Collecting picture postcards was a new activity which had to be catered for. Automatic vending machines sprang up on railway stations, beautiful boxes, inlaid cabinets and embossed albums were sold to hold cards and were displayed in the drawing room to impress the visitor. Magnifying glasses and minute ivory micro-viewers containing tiny postcard reproductions appeared. The postcard collection became an Edwardian social cachet. By 1903, the *Glasgow Evening Post* was complaining that 'in ten years time Europe will be buried beneath picture postcards'. Wrench Ltd produced cards of famous paintings, Raphael Tuck and Sons Ltd commissioned artists to paint views in their 'Oilette' series. Bamforth Ltd illustrated songs, hymns, views and music hall jokes. The interesting new aspect of this blossoming of the postcard industry was that unlike the pictorial stationery and the envelopes and souvenirs bought by the wealthy on the Grand Tour, here was an art form which, with cheaper travel and better education, could be enjoyed by almost everyone. The influence of German expertise on the burgeoning postcard industry cannot be underestimated. It was a German, Mr F. Hartmann who pressed the postal authorities to accept cards with a 'divided' back. With hindsight, this sounds a remarkably simple idea but there had been some confusion over the interpretation of previous postal regulations. With true business instinct, Mr Hartmann sent specimens of his cards to the Postmaster General for his approval. They had a line clearly drawn down the centre on one side. To the left of this was the message, and on the right of it the address, on the other side was the picture. The change was announced in the *Picture Postcard Magazine* in January 1902 which pointed out that 'Mr F Hartmann is the first publisher to take advantage of this concession . . .' and that at last a reasonably long message could be sent 'without spoiling the illustration'. Of course, the change was not immediate and it was some time before old stocks of undivided backs were used up but the new format began to appear later that year. France adopted it in 1904 and Germany in 1905. The Universal Postal Union did not adopt it until 1906, and Japan and the United States in 1907. Freedom for the postcard was assured. In 1914, over 800 million picture postcards were sent in Britain.

In the first decade of the century picture postcard
production became a new national industry but many
British firms were still dependent on German
marketing and printing techniques. It is significant
that the man responsible for setting Donald McGill
on the path towards a hitherto unknown job – that of
postcard artist – was Max Honnest-Reddlich, from
Germany.

Bibliography

ALDERSON, Frederick, *The Comic Postcard in English Life,* David & Charles, 1970.

ANDERSON, Janice & SWINGLEHURST, Edmund, *The Victorian and Edwardian Seaside,* Country Life Books, 1978.

BRIDGEMAN, H. & DRURY, Elizabeth, *Beside the Seaside,* Elm Tree Books, 1977.

BUCKLAND, Basil, N., *The World of Donald McGill,* 1976.

BYATT, Anthony, *Picture Postcards and their Publishers,* Golden Age Postcard Books, Malvern, 1978, and *Collecting Picture Postcards,* Malvern, 1982.

CALDER-MARSHALL, Arthur, *Wish you were here,* Hutchinson, 1966.

CARLINE, Richard, *Pictures in the Post,* Gordon Fraser Gallery, Ltd, 1971.

DÛVAL, William & MONAHAN, Valerie, *Collecting Postcards in Colour, 1894-1914,* Blandford Press, 1978.

GREEN, Benny, *I've Lost my Little Willie,* Elm Tree/Arrow Books, 1976.

HILL, C. W., *Discovering Picture Postcards,* Shire Publications, 1978.

HOLT, Tonie and Valmai, *Picture Postcards of the*

Golden Age – A Collector's Guide, MacGibbon & Kee, 1971.

HOWELL, Georgina, *The Penguin Book of Naughty Postcards,* Penguin Books, 1977.

KLAMKIN, Marian, *Picture Postcards,* David & Charles, 1974.

MONAHAN, Valerie, *Collecting Postcards in Colour, 1914-1930,* Blandford Press, 1980.

POUND, Reginald, *Maypole in the Strand,* Ernest Benn, 1948.

STAFF, Frank, *Picture Postcards & Travel, A Collector's Guide,* Lutterworth Press, 1979.

STAFF, Frank, *The Picture Postcard and it Origins,* Lutterworth Press, 1966.

WYKES, Alan, *Saucy Seaside Postcards,* Jupiter, 1977.

Illustration Credits

The copyright on the Donald McGill cards which are illustrated is held by Basil N. Buckland.

Thanks are due to Les Coleman for the loan of the following cards – 2, 10, 20, 87.

Thanks are also due to many others for their permission to reproduce cards.

List of Cards
Illustrated

Index